Flemish Giant Rabbits

The moral rights of the author has been asserted
British Library Cataloguing in Publication Data
A catalogue record for this book is available from the British Library

ISBN 978-1-909820-45-6

Disclaimer and Legal Notice

Flemish Giant Rabbits

A Pet Owner's Guide

How to Care for your Flemish Giant, including Health, Breeding, Personality, Lifespan, Colors, Diet, Facts and Clubs

Ann L. Fletcher

Foreword

Hello and thank you for buying my book.

In this book you will find some wonderful information to help you care for your Flemish Giant Rabbit. I've included in this book information about their care, habitat, cages, enclosure, diet, facts, set up, names, pictures, life span, breeding, feeding, cost and a care sheet. After reading this book you will be a lot more confident in looking after your Flemish Giant Rabbit!

I have written this book using American spelling as that is what I'm used to. I have given measurements in both feet and inches/pounds and ounces and also in metric. I have also given costs in US$ and GBP. Both the measurements and costs are approximate guides. I have done my best to ensure the accuracy of the information in this book as at the time of publishing.

I trust that after reading this book you will enjoy the experience of owning and looking after a Flemish Giant Rabbit and that you have a wonderful time enjoying the pleasure they bring in the years to come!

All good wishes, Ann L. Fletcher

Acknowledgements

I would like to thank my friend Macy for sharing with me her experiences of living with her Flemish Giant rabbit, Hagrid who has brought so much of pleasure and amusement to her family. It's amazing when I go to visit Macy, how much Hagrid is part of the household and you can't help laughing as he bounds around the room from one member of the family to the next.

Once again all my love and thanks to my husband John for his patience and understanding over the years. I couldn't have done it without him. A special thanks to my mom who has always supported me and encouraged me to write.

Table of Contents

Your Flemish Giant will also require a continuous
supply of clean fresh water usually provided for in a
water crock, tip-proof ceramic pet dish, or hanging
water bottle. It can be supplied using automatic
systems or by manually providing feed and/or water as

Chapter One: Introduction

There could be no more accurate name for this pet than "Flemish Giant Rabbit." While it is still a domestic rabbit breed, this breed of rabbit is much larger than the typical domestic rabbit – the term "giant" is entirely fitting. These rabbits can grow to the size of a medium-sized dog and they tend to exhibit many of the same personality traits as a dog – friendliness and loyalty included.

If you are looking for a kid-friendly household pet but don't want to go the conventional route of choosing a cat or dog, then the Flemish Giant Rabbit may make a superb alternative. These rabbits make wonderful pets because they are very docile and tend to be tolerant of handling. Not only does that make them a great option for you, but also for your children! These rabbits are quite unique in their size and appearance but they have all of the qualities you love in a cuddly new pet.

Before you buy a Flemish Giant Rabbit, you would do well to learn everything you can about the breed. Though these rabbits are very passive and friendly, they do require slightly different care than other domestic rabbits, especially in regard to cage size and feeding requirements.

If you want to ensure that your rabbit receives the best care possible, I hope you will find the facts I've provided helpful and informative. I trust that in reading my book, you will find the answers to your questions. I have included material I believe to be appropriate in assisting you in selecting and purchasing your rabbit as well as tips for housing, feeding and breeding your pet. By the time you finish this book I know you will feel a lot more confident and ready to provide excellent care for your Flemish Giant Rabbit!

Useful Terms to Know:

Buck – a male rabbit

Crown – refers to a prominent ridge and crest along the top of the head extending to the base of the ears

Dam – the mother of a rabbit

Dewlap – a flap of skin under the chin; seen in female rabbits

Doe – a female rabbit

Gestation period – the period between conception and birth; the period during which baby rabbits develop in the dam's womb

Hock – the joint of the rabbit's foot

Intermediate – Flemish Giant Rabbits from 6 to 8 months (show term)

Junior – Flemish Giant Rabbits up to 6 months (show term)

Kindling – the process of giving birth to young (kits)

Kit – a baby rabbit

Malocclusion – the misalignment of a rabbit's teeth

Pedigree – a record of the rabbit's lineage, generally reaching back at least 3 generations

Quick – the part of the nail that contains blood vessels and nerves; if severed, can cause pain and bleeding

Senior – All Flemish Giant Rabbits over 8 months with Does having a minimum weight requirement of 14 lbs. (6.35 kg) and Bucks a minimum of 13 lbs. (5.90 kg) (show term).

Sire – the father of a litter of rabbits

Solid – a rabbit with a single color covering the entire body

Weaning – the process of getting baby rabbits used to accepting solid food instead of their mother's milk

Chapter Two: Understanding Them

A t this point, you may not know anything about the Flemish Giant Rabbit other than the fact that it is one of the largest rabbit breeds out there. Before you decide whether or not it is the right pet for you, however, you should take the time to learn everything you can and perhaps compare it to the more standard breeds.

Only when you know all the details about the breed as well as its care requirements can you determine whether you are really able to provide for the needs of a Flemish Giant. In this section you will learn the basics about this wonderful breed as well as its history.

1.) What Are Flemish Giant Rabbits?

The Flemish Giant Rabbit is exactly what it sounds like – it is a domestic rabbit known for its large size. While many pet rabbits reach a maximum weight under 10 lbs. (4.54 kg), the Flemish Giant averages between 14 and 18 lbs. (6.35 to 8.16 kg) at maturity. These rabbits have long, powerful bodies that can reach 32 inches (81.3 cm) or more in length. When standing upright on its hind legs, these rabbits can be 3 feet (91.4 cm) tall!

Like most rabbits, this breed comes in a variety of colors – the ARBA recognizes and accounts for seven different colors in the breed standard. These colors are: black, blue, fawn, light grey, sandy, steel grey and white. What sets these rabbits apart from other domestic rabbits is, of course, their impressive size. Another unique feature of these rabbits, however, is their gentility – the Flemish Giant is often nicknamed the "gentle giant" because they are so compliant and tolerant of handling. If you are looking for a unique family pet, then the Flemish Giant Rabbit is an inspired choice.

2.) Facts about Flemish Giant Rabbits

The Flemish Giant Rabbit is one of many domestic rabbit breeds. Down through the centuries rabbits have been bred for a variety of different reasons – for meat, fur or more commonly today, simply as pets. In addition to their size, the docility of the Flemish Giant sets it apart from other domestic breeds and makes it a particularly good house pet – they also tend to get along with cats and dogs.

In regard to the appearance of the Flemish Giant, these rabbits have long and powerful bodies. They are well muscled with broad, muscular hindquarters. Males of the breed tend to have broader heads than females and females tend to sport a large, full dewlap under the chin. A dewlap is simply a fold of skin under the chin of the rabbit. The coat of this breed is dense and glossy – when stroked, the fur will roll back to its original position.

The size of Flemish Giant Rabbits varies greatly depending on breeding. Both the American Rabbit Breeders Association (ARBA) and the British Rabbit Council (BRC) have standards for the minimum weight of Flemish Giants for show. The ARBA states that the minimum weight for a senior Doe is 14 lbs. (6.35 kg) and the minimum for a senior Buck is 13 lbs. (5.90 kg). The BRC, on the other hand, states that Does should be no less than 12 lbs. (5.44 kg) and Bucks no less than 11 lbs. (4.99 kg). Because size varies according to breeding, neither governing body mandates a maximum weight for Flemish Giant Rabbits.

The length and height of Flemish Giant Rabbits varies by sex and age. At maturity, however, these rabbits can stand up to 3 feet (91.4 cm) tall on their hind legs though the average height of this breed, when standing on all four legs, is about 16 to 18 inches (40.6 to 45.7 cm). As is to be expected given their overall size, Flemish Giant Rabbits also have very large ears. The ARBA states that the ears should measure at least 5.25 inches (13.3 cm).

Fun Facts about Flemish Giants

- They are often referred to as "gentle giants" due to their docility

- Also nicknamed the "King of Rabbits" due to its size

- They are the top breed for show and are often seen in 4-H club shows

- They are the second oldest domesticated breed in the United States

- A Flemish Giant may sit on your lap like a pet dog would do

- Benny, a Flemish Giant from Oxfordshire, holds the record as the longest rabbit at 32 inches (81.3 cm)

Summary of Facts

Classification: pet breed

Weight: 14 to 18 lbs. (6.35 to 8.16 kg) at maturity

Length: up to 32 inches (81.3 cm)

Height on all 4 legs: 16 to 18 inches (40.6 to 45.7 cm)

Body Shape: long with broad hindquarters

Body Structure: powerful with good muscular development; females have a dewlap

Coat: dense and glossy, rolls back

Coat Color: black, blue, fawn, light grey, sandy, steel grey or white (accepted by ARBA)

Temperament: docile and tolerant of handling

Lifespan: average 5 to 7 years

Other Pets: gets along well with cats and dogs

3.) History of Flemish Giant Rabbits as Pets

The Flemish Giant Rabbit is widely regarded as one of the oldest breeds of domestic rabbit and it continues to remain one of the most popular breeds for show. As the name suggests, these rabbits originated in the Flanders region of Northern Belgium, possibly as early as the 16th century. Though exact details are unknown, it is thought that the breed is descended from meat and fur breeds – possibly the Steenkonijn and/or the European Patagonian which is now extinct and not associated with the South American variety.

Some sources claim that during the 16th and 17th centuries, Dutch sailors brought specimens of the Patagonian rabbit from the Patagonia region of Chile and Argentina back with them from their trading in South America to Europe. The belief is that it was sold for meat and bred with local rabbits to eventually produce the Flemish Giant. It seems unlikely however, as the Patagonian rabbit is a wild species of rabbit and weighs less than 2 lbs. (about 0.91 kg), nor is the Patagonian hare a possibility as it is a species in the cavy family of rodents that cannot interbreed with rabbits.

The earliest record of the Flemish Giant didn't occur until about 1860. It was during this time that rumors of a giant rabbit were circulating throughout Europe, carried by travelers. Though these rabbits were reported to weigh between 18 and 20 lbs. (8.16 to 9.72 kg), specimens of the breed averaged closer to 12 to 14 lbs. (5.44 to 6.35 kg). The size of this breed became particularly significant to English breeders of meat rabbit stock – they typically produced meat from rabbits weighing only 7 to 8 lbs. (3.18 to 3.63 kg).

Early specimens of the Flemish Giant breed that were exhibited in show were very large, but not necessarily attractive. It wasn't until 1893 that a standard for the breed was published. At this time, the average specimen of the breed was a dirty grey in color with long ears bent at the tips. With increased interest in rabbit breeding as a fancy, however, the appearance of the breed began to improve. Modern specimens are now known for their impressive size as well as their beautiful coloration.

Around the same time the standards for the breed were published, the Flemish Giant was exported from England and Belgium to America. It wasn't until 1910, however, that the breed began to gain popularity. In 1915, the National Federation of Flemish Giant Rabbit Breeders was founded in the United States with the goal of promoting and improving the breed. The other breed club in the United States is the Eastern States Flemish Giant Rabbit Breeders Association. All these clubs provide valuable information to breeders and owners for the protection and promotion of the Flemish Giant Breed.

Over time, the Flemish Giant has become a favorite among breeders, leading in number of exhibitions at principle shows. Selling prices for this breed are also among the highest of all popular domestic rabbit breeds.

a.) History of the ARBA

The American Rabbit Breeders' Association (ARBA) was founded in 1910 and has its headquarters in Bloomington, Illinois. The purpose of this association is to promote rabbit fancy and to facilitate commercial rabbit production. The ARBA is responsible for setting breed standards and sanctioning rabbit shows throughout North America. In addition to sponsoring local clubs and fairs, the ARBA holds a national convention show annually, drawing rabbit fanciers from around the globe.

Not only does the ARBA set breed standards and organize shows, it also serves to provide rabbit raising education. Every five years the ARBA publishes a detailed guide for rabbit fanciers called *Standard of Perfection*. The ARBA also publishes educational materials like guidebooks and posters including photographs of all the recognized rabbit breeds. Additionally, the ARBA has a library of over 10,000 books and writings on domestic rabbits – the largest single repository of its kind.

b.) History of the BRC

The breeding and showing of rabbits began over two hundred years ago. Throughout the nineteenth century, fanciers gathered to form local clubs for showing and improving individual breeds. The number of rabbit breeds recognized increased throughout the 1800s and early 1900s but by 1918, the most popular breed by far was the Beveren. In May of 1918 breeders of Beveren rabbits gathered to form a national club called The Beveren Club.

The Beveren Club served to raise the profile of rabbit breeding, adopting and standardizing new breeds. Eventually, the name of the club changed to the British Fur Rabbit Society and then to the British Rabbit Society. By 1928, over a dozen different breeds were recognized and interest in rabbit breeding began to grow. As a result, a new club was formed called the National Rabbit Council of Great Britain. The club grew quickly but conflicts arose between the two clubs which led to them eventually merging in 1934 to form the British Rabbit Council.

c.) History of the National Federation of Flemish Giant Rabbit Breeders

The NFFGRB (www.nffgrb.net) was founded on November 4th, 1915 when four Flemish Giant Rabbit breeders met in Denver, CO. Over the next year, officers were appointed and the secretary and president of the club (Bill Taylor and Lewis S. J. Griffin, respectively) met to create the first Federation Standard. At that time, the only colors recognized were light gray, steel and black – thus, the first standard for the breed only covered these colors.

In 1916, the first officially sanctioned Flemish shows were held and, during that same year, the first Flemish Federation Year Book was published. In addition to information about the breed and relevant pictures, this book also contained the constitution, by-laws, show rules and standards applicable to the club and to the Flemish Giant breed. By 1917, the club had become a branch association of the National Breeders and Fanciers Association of America.

In 1921, the Ashtabula Ohio Flemish Rabbit Breeders Association was formed, becoming the first Flemish Specialty Club. By the end of the year, several other specialty clubs had formed including the Mississippi Valley Flemish Breeders, the Indiana Flemish Breeders Association and the Boosters Association of St. Louis, MO. Many shows were held over the next few years and membership in these clubs climbed steadily.

By 1924, a new color variation for the Flemish Giant was accepted by the Federation. This new color, sandy gray (also called natural at the time), was added to the breed standard. The term "natural" was eventually dropped, and the color sandy gray is one of the seven colors still accepted by the Federation today. Ten years later, in 1934, the breed standard was edited and published again, but the changes were minimal and stayed in effect until another review and rewriting occurred in 1979.

In 1979, the Eastern States Flemish Giant Rabbit Breeders Association was formed with 14 charter members. In the years that followed, membership had grown to over 100 and it has become one of the premier Flemish Giant specialty clubs in the nation. In 2002, the West Coast Flemish Giant Club was formed, serving to unite Flemish Giant fanciers and breeders in the states of the Pacific Time Zone in the United States.

d.) United States Flemish Giant Clubs

The clubs listed below are specialty breed clubs affiliated with the ARBA:

- Eastern States Flemish Giant Rabbit Breeders Association (2812 Dinnerbell Five Forks, Farmington, PA 15437) http://esfgrba.webs.com

- Iowa Flemish Giant Rabbit Club (304 W. Columbus St, Crawfordsville, IA 52621)http://ifgra.tripod.com

- Midwest Flemish Giant Rabbit Club (11601 Maries Rd 302, Vienna, MO 63377)

- Southern Flemish Giant Rabbit Club (323 Macedon Dr, Lexington, SC 29073) www.southernflemish.yolasite.com

- Upper Midwest Flemish Giant Club (9054 120th Ave, Bloomer, WI 54724)

e.) United Kingdom Flemish Giant Clubs

The clubs listed below are specialty breed clubs affiliated with the BRC:

- National Flemish Giant Rabbit Club www.thebrc.org/clubs-national.htm

- National British Giant Rabbit Association http://nbgra.webs.com

4.) Colors of Flemish Giants

Like most domestic rabbits, the Flemish Giant comes in a variety of different colors. The American Rabbit Breeders Association (ARBA) identifies seven acceptable colors in Flemish Giant Rabbits: black, blue, fawn, light gray, sandy, steel, gray and white.

I've listed on the following pages a brief explanation of each color:

Black

The surface color of the rabbit is black with an undercoat of slate blue. Rabbits with black coats should have brown eyes. Ticking or a brown cast to the coat will be considered a fault in this variety.

Blue

The surface color of the rabbit is dark blue with an undercoat of slate blue. The eyes are blue-gray in color. Ticking ear lacing and a brownish cast to the coat will be considered a fault in this variety.

Fawn

The surface color of the rabbit is a golden straw color with an undercoat blending to a pale cream color. The belly and underside of the tail may range from light cream to white – crotch marks are acceptable. Rabbits with fawn coats should have brown eyes. Ticking, patches on the body, ear lacing, red belly and excessively wide eye circles are considered faults in this variety.

Light Gray

The surface of the rabbit is light gray in color with black-tipped guard hairs. The coat is agouti with banding becoming distinct when the coat is blowing. The undercoat is slate blue with an immediate band of off-white color. The belly and underside of the tail are white – crotch marks are acceptable. The eyes should be brown. Faults include dark grey belly and sandiness in surface color.

Sandy

The surface color is a reddish, sand color with dark, contrasting ticking. The undercoat has a brassy immediate color with slate blue coloring next to the skin. The ears are laced with black, the eyes brown. The belly and underside of the tail are cream to white – crotch marks are acceptable. Faults include heavy ticking and patch color.

Steel Gray

The surface color is a black, steel gray with evenly distributed light gray-tipped guard hairs. The color is uniform over the entire body. The undercoat is slate blue, the belly color white – crotch marks are acceptable. The eyes should be brown. Faults include a brownish cast to the fur, black patches or belly color too similar to the body.

White

The rabbit should be pure white in color throughout. The eyes are pink. Faults in this variety include staining on the coat and yellow case.

Chapter Three: What to Know Before You Buy

If, after reading the last chapter, you still feel like the Flemish Giant Rabbit is the right pet for you, congratulations! Before you rush out and buy one, however, there are a few practical things you should know about the breed.

In this chapter I will make reference to licensing regulations, keeping these rabbits with other pets and look at the costs involved in providing a safe habitat and caring for your Flemish Giant Rabbit. This should reassure you that you are then fully prepared to get your own giant!

1.) Do You Need a License?

Licensing for pets is typically limited to dogs and cats as well as "exotic" pets. In regard to domestic rabbits, however, the thought of licensing your rabbit may never have even occurred to you. Before you purchase and bring home your rabbit, however, it would be wise for you to determine the licensing requirements for the area in which you live. These requirements vary from one region to another and from one country to another, so be sure to research the regulations specific to your area.

a.) Licensing in the U.S.

There is no federal law in the United States requiring private rabbit owners to obtain a license for keeping Flemish Giant Rabbits. There are, however, certain state laws regarding the keeping and breeding of domestic rabbits. The state of Minnesota, for example, requires rabbit owners to pay a $15 (£9.75) annual fee to license their pet rabbit – a higher fee may be charged if the rabbit is not spayed or neutered.

Generally, retail pet store owners and private collectors are not required to obtain a permit for keeping Flemish Giant Rabbits. If you plan to breed your rabbits for wholesale or exhibition, however, you may need to obtain a license. To determine the requirements for your particular area, check with your local council. It is better to be safe than sorry – especially if failing to license your rabbit could cost you hefty fines.

b.) Licensing in the U.K.

The U.K. does not have any legislation requiring rabbit owners or breeders to obtain a license. There are, however, laws in place in regard to importing or exporting animals. Rabies has long been eradicated from the U.K. and strict import and export laws are now in place to prevent the disease from being re-introduced. If you plan to bring a rabbit with you to the U.K., or if you plan to export one, you will need to obtain an animal movement license (AML).

c.) Licensing Elsewhere

Licensing requirements for Flemish Giant Rabbits vary from one country or region to another. One of the only cases in which the ownership of pet rabbits is expressly prohibited is in Queensland, Australia.

Rabbits are not a native species in Queensland – they are actually considered a Class 2 pest by the Land Protection Act of 2002. A penalty of Australian $44,000 can be levied as a result of flaunting this law.

As they are not a native species, rabbits can threaten the survival of certain native species and also cause damage to the environment. You cannot obtain a license to keep a pet rabbit in Queensland because it is illegal. The only time in which a permit may be issued is if the rabbit is being used for research or entertainment purposes.

2.) How Many Should You Buy?

The Flemish Giant Rabbit is a very docile breed and these animals can bond well with members of the family. As long as you provide your rabbit with adequate attention and exercise, you shouldn't need more than one rabbit. In fact, some rabbits simply do not get along with other rabbits. This is particularly true if you try to keep two intact males together in the same cage – they are likely to fight violently, possibly causing serious injury.

When compared to most other breeds, they do have a very relaxed and easy going personality with the Buck on the whole being more inquisitive and tolerant of people. The Doe however, can be prone to be more territorial and moody especially when breeding or when looking after her litter.

If you plan to keep more than one Flemish Giant, limit it to one fixed Buck and one Doe or two Does. You should also think about the size of a Flemish Giant Rabbit – do you have the space and resources to care for more than one? These are important questions that need to be answered before you buy as they will have a big impact on your home and family, in addition to the financial implications involved. You could end up with a lot more bunny than you bargained for!

3.) Can They Be Kept with Other Pets?

The true answer to this question varies depending on the personality and temperament of the individual rabbit and the pets that they are mixing with. For the most part, however, Flemish Giants tend to get along very well with other pets including cats and dogs. In fact, these rabbits often grow to be larger than most cats and the same size as small to medium-sized dogs, so you don't have to worry about your pet regarding itself as prey!

However, you should take some precautions and always supervise its time with other pets to prevent any accidents. It is important to make sure your Gentle Giant has a safe place to retreat to if it wants to and avoid him having access to food belonging to other pets in the family.

A word of caution in respect of ferrets which are predatory animals and may injure your rabbit and birds which depending on the species could irritate your rabbit due to their sensitive ears.

If you have pets kept in tanks (e. g. fish and frogs), please ensure that your rabbit does not chew on electrical cords. This would obviously apply to any electrical cords throughout your home.

4.) Ease and Cost of Care

Before you commit to a Flemish Giant, you need to be sure you can provide for the basic needs of your new pet. In addition to buying the rabbit itself, you also need to purchase a cage, basic supplies and enough food to get your rabbit started. After you cover these initial costs, you then have to think about regular monthly costs involved in keeping your rabbit such as bedding, food, replacements of toys and veterinary costs.

In this section I've outlined the initial costs and monthly costs of keeping a Flemish Giant Rabbit as a rough guide so that you have an understanding of what to expect.

a.) Initial Costs

The initial costs for a Flemish Giant include those costs that are necessary to prepare for and bring your rabbit home. These may include the purchase price, cost of the cage, spay/neuter surgery and cage accessories. Below you will find an overview of each cost.

Purchase Price: The price of Flemish Giant Rabbit will vary depending where you buy it. You may be able to find these rabbits at your local pet store but I strongly recommend you purchase them from a reputable breeder for around $40 to $100 (£26 to £65).

Spay/Neuter: If you do not plan to breed your rabbit, it may be a good idea to have your Flemish Giant spayed or neutered. I would recommend that you speak to your veterinarian for advice regarding this. The cost of spay/neuter surgery is generally around $100 (£65) but prices will vary from area to area.

Microchipping: A microchip is a tiny electronic device that is inserted under your rabbit's skin. This device is used to store your contact information so if the rabbit is lost, you can be contacted. It is not a requirement that you have your rabbit microchipped, but it is certainly a good idea. The cost of this procedure is generally about $30 (£19.50).

Vaccinations: In the United States, vaccinations are not required for pet rabbits – you may, however, still choose to get them. In the UK, vaccinations for myxomatosis and viral hemorrhagic disease are recommended. Costs for veterinary care may vary depending where you live but the average cost for initial vaccinations is around $50 (£32.50). I strongly recommend that you check with your veterinarian regarding which vaccinations are recommended in your local area.

Cage: Because Flemish Giant Rabbits are so large, they need a significant amount of space. It is always a good idea to keep the motto "bigger is better" in mind when purchasing a cage for a Flemish Giant because it is much better to have more space than your rabbit needs than it is to not have enough. The cost for a cage will vary depending on size and materials, but you should be ready to spend around $200 to $300 (£130 to £195).

Accessories: To prepare your rabbit's cage you will need to stock up on a few accessories. These accessories might include a water bottle, food bowl, bedding, litter pan and chew toys for your rabbit. Another accessory that would be good to have around is a travel carrier – this will be useful when you need to take your rabbit to the vet.

For Flemish Giant Rabbits in particular, you will also need to purchase a slicker brush to groom your rabbit several times a week. The cost of initial accessories may be around $75 (£48.75).

Summary of Initial Costs		
Cost Type	One Rabbit	Two Rabbits
Purchase Price	$40 to $100 (£26 to £65)	$80 to $200 (£52 to £130)
Spay/Neuter	$100 (£65)	$200 (£130)
Microchipping	$30 (£19.50)	$60 (£39)
Vaccinations	$50 (£32.50)	$100 (£65)
Cage or Pen	$200 to $300 (£130 to £195)	$200 to $300 (£130 to £195)
Cage Accessories	$75 (£48.75)	$75 (£48.75)
Total:	$495 to $655 (£321.75 to £425.75)	$715 to $935 (£464.75 to £607.75)

b.) Monthly Costs

In addition to the initial costs, you also have to think about the monthly costs to keep one. These costs will include food, bedding, replacement toys and regular veterinary care. Below you will find an explanation of and an estimate for each cost.

Food: Your monthly costs for rabbit food will vary depending how many rabbits you keep and what type of food you buy. Some of the types of food you will need to buy for your rabbits include greens, hay, commercial rabbit pellets and fresh vegetables. Flemish Giant Rabbits have a strong appetite and can eat up to 1 ½ cups (345 g) of food per day. Thus, the cost to feed a single Flemish Giant for one month (including hay, pellets and vegetables) averages about $50 to $75 (£32.50 to £48.75).

Bedding: No matter where you keep you rabbit whether in its cage or hutch, or if you are relaxed and have him roam free throughout the house, you will need to provide him a 'safe' place he can call his own. In terms of bedding, the best kinds to use are non-toxic pelleted litter, fresh hay or newspaper. Pine and cedar shavings can cause irritation and both clay and clumping cat litters can be harmful to rabbits.

Your monthly cost for bedding will also depend on the type of bedding you buy. In general, you should plan to spend up to $20 (£13) per month on bedding. You can reduce your bedding costs by using recycled newspapers, but do not use colored magazines because the ink may contain toxins that are harmful to your rabbit if he eats it. No matter what type of bedding you choose, be sure to replace it often even if it doesn't look like it needs it.

Veterinary Care: If you care for your Flemish Giant properly, you should not have to worry about veterinary care on a monthly basis. You should, however, take your rabbit to the vet for a check-up once a year. The total yearly cost for this is generally around $50 (£32.50) which averages to less than $5 (£3.25) per month.

Additional Costs: Other monthly costs you should be prepared for include replacing chew toys and making repairs to the cage or supplies. Because many owners choose to keep their Flemish Giants out of the cage during the day, your rabbit's cage may not experience a great deal of wear-and-tear. The costs described are generally not very high and may only be $60 (£39) per year which is $5 (£3.25) per month.

Summary of Monthly Costs		
Cost Type	One Rabbit	Two Rabbits
Food	$50 to $75 (£32.50 to £48.75)	$100 to $150 (£65 to £97.50)
Bedding	$20 (£13)	$40 (£26)
Veterinary Care	$5 (£3.25)	$10 (£6.50)
Additional Costs	$5 (£3.25)	$10 (£6.50)
Total:	$80 to $105 (£52 to £68.25)	$160 to $210 (£104 to £136.50)

c.) Estimate of Time Required

Flemish Giant Rabbits are no different from any other pet in the sense that you must set aside a certain portion of your time every day and every week to care for them. I've listed below some of the tasks you should expect to perform in caring for your Gentle Giant:

Daily Tasks:

- Cleaning out and refilling water bottle
- Cleaning out and refilling food dish/hay rack
- Offering your rabbit fresh vegetables
- Checking your rabbit's eyes, ears, teeth, etc.
- Provide supervised time to play outside the cage
- Offer interaction and play time with your rabbit

Estimated Time Commitment: 1 hour per day minimum

Weekly Tasks:

- Clean out the cage and refresh the bedding
- Wash any toys your rabbit regularly uses
- Brush your rabbit's coat with a slicker brush several times weekly

- Clean out the rabbit's litter box as needed (several times per week)

Estimated Time Commitment: 10 hours per week

5.) Human Health Considerations

Before you buy, you also need to consider any implications to your and your families own health. For example, do you know if you have an allergy or sensitivity to rabbits? I would recommend taking advice from your Doctor to ensure that you understand the implications to your own health and if necessary, are allergy tested.

6.) Pros and Cons of Flemish Giant Rabbits

The Flemish Giant Rabbit makes a wonderful pet, but it may not be the right pet for everyone. Before you go out and buy a Flemish Giant, I've listed some of the benefits of having a smaller breed of rabbit along with the pros and cons of the breed itself, which hopefully will assist you in making an informed decision should you choose whether or not to buy one of these gentle giants.

Most of the other popular breeds of rabbits require a far smaller size of cage and typically, though not always, are kept in their cage for the most part with some free time in the house. They adapt well to outdoor hutches allowing for the climate of where you live and generally have little trouble keeping themselves clean. There are exceptions as with the Angora rabbit that requires a lot of additional care. A big difference in monthly expenditure is in respect of their food bill which will be a lot lower. As they are smaller animals, duties such as trimming nails and grooming will be a lot easier and straightforward.

Pros of the Flemish Giant

- Very docile and tolerant of handling
- Tends to get along well with other household pets (cats and dogs)
- Can easily be litter trained – reduces some of the hassle of cleaning
- Come in a variety of colors – 7 accepted by the ARBA
- One of the most popular breeds for rabbit shows
- Typically given free reign of the home, not kept in a cage at all times but does require its own space at night
- Very friendly breed, bonds closely with owners if properly cared for
- Can be a good choice for older children if they are educated in the proper handling of the rabbit

Cons of the Flemish Giant

- Much larger than other rabbit breeds – requires significant space Minimum cage size is 30 by 72 inches (76.2 by 182.9 cm)

- May not get along with other rabbits – two males shouldn't be kept together

- Might not react well to small children – powerful legs and sharp claws can be dangerous

- Require significantly more food than smaller rabbit breeds –this will increase the cost of feeding them

- Not ideal for keeping in a hutch – require a lot of space and protection from the weather

- Due to its size, it will have difficulty grooming itself so will require more grooming than smaller breeds - must purchase a slicker brush for this purpose

- Extra caution needed when trimming nails due to size and powerful hind legs (may require the help of a second person)

- Do not tolerate hot weather well – prone to overheating

Chapter Four: Purchasing Flemish Giant Rabbits

If having got this far you have decided that the Flemish Giant Rabbit is indeed the right pet for you, you will probably be quite excited at the prospect of heading out to buy one.

Before you do, it is imperative that you perform some basic research and give due consideration to your options to ensure that you get a happy and healthy rabbit.

The last thing you want to do is to bring home a rabbit just to find out that it is already sick – it is heartbreaking to lose a new pet. In this chapter I've noted some of the key points to consider along with some valuable tips about where to get a Flemish Giant Rabbit and how to pick out one that is healthy.

1.) Where to Buy Flemish Giant Rabbits

When you decide that a Flemish Giant Rabbit is definitely the right choice for you and your family, you then have the challenge of finding one! When it comes to buying rabbits, you have several options to choose from.

Because this breed is not one of the most common rabbit breeds, my recommendation is to source your pet from an independent breeder. If you plan to breed your rabbits or train them for show, you should definitely purchase from an independent breeder in any event. Below you will find valuable resources to help you find your new pet.

a.) Buying in the U.S.

You should not expect to be able to walk into your local pet store and find a Flemish Giant Rabbit. They will probably stock some of the more common breeds of domestic rabbit, but they will see this breed as a bit of an exotic. Even if the pet store does have some available, you should not necessarily buy one without shopping around first. In buying from a pet store, you do not necessarily know where the rabbit came from and unlikely that they will have any information about its genetics and family history.

The safest option for finding a Flemish Giant Rabbit is to go to a breeder. This way your rabbit will be less likely to get sick or have temperament problems. You also have the comfort of knowing that you have an expert you can call on if you have any questions, or if you run into problems with your rabbit.

You can find local breeders by performing an online search or if you are feeling cheeky, you can ask your local pet store or better still your local veterinarian for a referral. Once you find a breeder, make sure you ask plenty of questions to ascertain the breeder's experience and to ensure that the rabbit you bring home is healthy. A good breeder will also want to ensure you are the right owner for one of its rabbits and will no doubt want to satisfy themselves that you are fully aware of the commitment and responsibility you are taking on.

Try some of these resources to find a breeder:

National Federation of Flemish Giant Rabbit Breeders
www.nffgrb.net/Breeders.htm

Flemish Giant Rabbit Breeders.

http://rabbitbreeders.us/flemish-giant-rabbits

Eastern States Flemish Giant Rabbit Breeders Association.

http://esfgrba.webs.com

Another option which I totally applaud is to adopt a rabbit from a local rabbit rescue. If you are interested in this route, try some of these resources to find one:

Diana's Rabbit Rescue.

http://dianasrabbitrescue.info/Rabbit_Rescue_Meet_The_Bunnies.htm

Georgia House Rabbit Society.

www.houserabbitga.com/?tag=flemish-giant

Hug-a-Bunny Rabbit Rescue, Inc.

http://hugabunnyrabbitrescue.blogspot.com/2009/11/welcome-back-angelina.html

b.) Buying in the U.K.

The options for buying a Flemish Giant Rabbit in the UK are fairly similar to the U.S. Again, you are unlikely to find one for sale at your local pet store, but there are of course exceptions but my guidance as to its origin, genetics and family background still apply. Shop around a bit and take the time to find some local breeders as this should prove the better option long term.

Try some of these resources to find a breeder:

Singleton Stud – British & Continental Giant Rabbits.
www.british-giantrabbits.co.uk

Flemish Giant Rabbit Breeders.
http://rabbitbreeders.org.uk/flemish-giant-rabbit-breeders

Fieldview Stud Specialist Breeder.
www.fieldview-rabbits.co.uk

Again, in the UK adopting from a local rabbit rescue is also another option. If you are interested in this as a possibility, try some of these resources to find one:

The Rabbit Residence Rescue.
www.rabbitresidence.org.uk

Cotton Tails Rescue.
http://cottontails-rescue.org.uk

Rabbit Rehome.
www.rabbitrehome.org.uk/breeds.asp

2.) How to Select a Healthy Flemish Giant Rabbit

Don't be one of those owners who brings home a rabbit just to find out that it is sick. Unfortunately, many inexperienced rabbit owners make the mistake of purchasing a Flemish Giant without first gauging its health level. Once you purchase a rabbit, you may not be able to return it if consequently you find out it has health problems – by that point, you are likely to have already bonded with the rabbit and will be reluctant to return it anyway.

Do not be tempted to think that you are doing the rabbit a kindness by taking home one that has obvious health issues – it will just be a lot of headache and heartache for you in the long run and the rabbit may not even live very long. Do yourself a favor and take the time to make sure that the rabbit you bring home is in good condition.

Follow these tips to bring home a healthy rabbit:

1. Do your research before picking a breeder and buying a rabbit

2. Take a tour of the facilities

3. Observe and examine the rabbit kits individually

4. Make your choice and start the process

Do your research.

Shop around for a reputable breeder and take the time to interview each breeder. Nothing beats a personal recommendation and someone who has been in business for a long time will be there because of a good track record. If meeting someone unknown, then ask questions to ascertain the breeder's knowledge of and experience with the Flemish Giant Breed. If the breeder can't answer your questions or appears to be avoiding them, move on to another breeder.

Ask for a tour.

Once you select a breeder, it is always a good idea to pay a visit to the facilities. Ask to see the places where the rabbits are kept and ask to see the parents of the litter from which you are buying. If the facilities are dirty or the parents appear to be in poor health, do not purchase a rabbit from that breeder, thank them for their time and move on.

Observe the kits.

If the facilities and parents appear to be in good order, ask to see the litter of rabbits. Observe their appearance and activity to see if they look healthy. Healthy Flemish Giant Rabbits should be active and curious, not hiding in a corner or acting lethargically.

Examine the rabbits individually.

If the litter appears to be in good condition, pick out a few of the rabbits that you like. Ask for permission to handle the rabbits briefly to see how they react to human interaction and check them for obvious signs of disease and injury. Check the rabbit's ears and nose for discharge and make sure that the eyes are bright and clear. The rabbit's teeth should be straight and its coat healthy.

While the Flemish Giant has certain characteristics, each rabbit is still an individual with its own personality and behavioral oddities. Take your time to ensure you are happy before committing yourself to bring him home. He will be part of your life for many years.

If, after touring the facilities and ensuring that the rabbits themselves are healthy, you can begin to make negotiations with the breeder. Make sure you get the rabbit's medical history and breeding information for your own records. Ask if the rabbit comes with a health guarantee and make sure you get all the paperwork necessary to register your rabbit, should you choose to do so. A good breeder is someone to keep in touch with, for if you have any concerns or worries, they are generally only too delighted to pass on their wisdom and knowledge. They will love their rabbits and will be delighted that you are a caring and interested enough to go back to them for advice.

Chapter Five: Caring for Flemish Giant Rabbits

Like any other pet you bring home, a Flemish Giant Rabbit becomes your new friend and responsibility as soon as you bring him inside your house. That being the case, it is up to you to provide him with the best care you possibly can.

In this chapter I will cover the basics about providing for your rabbit's needs in regards to housing and feeding. You will also receive tips for handling your rabbit. Flemish Giants are much larger than other domestic breeds, so they have unique needs in terms of habitat and feeding requirements.

1.) Habitat Requirements

Before you bring your Flemish Giant Rabbit home, you need to be sure you can provide for its basic needs. Not only do you need to think about things like food and water, but you also need to have a place to put your rabbit. Many rabbit owners allow their pets to run around the house during the day, but you also still need a safe place to put them at night and where they will feel secure. In the following sections, you will learn the requirements you need to meet in providing your rabbit with a suitable living area.

a.) Need for Space

Because they are so large, the number one requirement in terms of a habitat for Flemish Giant Rabbits is space. The very minimum cage size for one of these rabbits is 30 by 72 inches (76.2 by 182.9 cm), but in my opinion bigger is always better and minimum sizes should be ignored. If you are planning on breeding your rabbits, a cage for a pregnant Doe and her litter should be a minimum of 60 by 96 inches (152.4 by 243.8 cm). Again, please note these are minimum sizes and not what I would recommend. How big? The biggest you can comfortably fit. Not only does the pregnant female require space to stretch out and move around contentedly, but you also need extra space for the kits when they are born.

Another factor you need to consider in selecting a cage for your Flemish Giant is the cage height. These rabbits have naturally erect ears but, if the cage ceiling isn't high enough, they may not carry their ears properly. The minimum cage height recommended for these rabbits is 24 inches (61 cm). If you are building your own cage or using a rabbit hutch, this shouldn't be an issue. With commercially-produced rabbit cages, however, you should check the height of the cage before you buy.

Instead of buying a large cage, it might be worth considering if at all possible, setting aside a room in your home just for your Flemish Giant. Another alternative is using larger dog crates which due to their size would be more suitable than conventional rabbit cages. In the United States, the Department of Agriculture has a standard that states that rabbits over 12 lbs. (5.44 kg) must have at least 5 square feet of floor space.

b.) Other Considerations

Though the size of the cage is the most important consideration for your Flemish Giant Rabbit, it is not the only thing to think about. You also need to think about the materials from which it is made and the floor of the cage. If you choose to house your rabbit outdoors, you will most likely use a rabbit hutch made of wood. These hutches are a viable option as long as you take precautions to protect your rabbit against the extremes of weather and temperature (both hot and cold).

Commercially-produced rabbit cages are typically made of galvanized wire. These cages are a good choice because wire walls are able to breathe better than solid walls. They also help your rabbit from ingesting any paint or vinyl coating if it chews on them. One thing to be wary of, however, is wire floors. If the floor of your rabbit's cage is wire, it could cause your rabbit to develop sores on his feet – due to their weight Flemish Giant Rabbits are particularly prone to developing this problem, so wire floors are not recommended for this breed.

The two best options for the floor of your rabbit cage are wooden slats or solid floors covered with bedding. Wooden slats allow waste to drop through the floor of the cage so the rabbit will not be sitting / laying in it. If you choose to use wooden slats, they should be spaced about 5/8 of an inch (1.6 cm) apart, each measuring about 1 inch (2.5 cm) wide. If you go the other route, line the floor of your rabbit's cage with straw, shredded paper or shredded wood chips. Bedding will not only make the bottom of your rabbit's cage soft, but it will also help to absorb liquid to keep your rabbit dry in between cage cleanings. All materials used should of course be non-toxic. Remember that their bedding should be changed often (at least every 3 days) to remove any build up of waste and odor and help prevent disease, while also keeping their fur free of waste material that may accumulate on their bodies.

A unique feature of keeping a Flemish Giant as a pet is the fact that they are very similar to dogs in many ways. Not only are these rabbits the size of a small to medium-sized dog, but they also have a friendly, dog-like temperament. This being the case, many Flemish Giant Rabbit owners choose to give their rabbit free reign of the house rather than keeping him in a cage all the time. You should still have a cage or area for your rabbit to sleep in at night, of course, but Flemish Giant Rabbits in particular do well given free space to run around in the home during the day.

c.) Cage Accessories

In addition to providing your rabbit with a home of the proper size and material, you also need to provide a few basics. Your rabbit will need a large water bottle to provide it with access to unlimited fresh water. Plan to clean and refill the water at least once per day and check the water level often so your rabbit doesn't run out. For your rabbit's food pellets, you will need a ceramic dish that doesn't take up too much space in the cage. A ceramic dish is recommended because it is heavy enough that your rabbit won't be likely to knock it over, and it will be easy to keep clean. Stainless steel dishes are also a good option because they don't tend to harbor bacteria.

Rabbits tend to eat a lot of roughage in addition to their pellet food. To give your rabbit access to hay, equip your rabbit's cage with a hay rack or wheel. These devices keep the hay up off the floor of the cage where it won't be soiled so your rabbit has clean food to eat. In addition to a hay rack, you should also provide your rabbit with a few chew toys and he might enjoy cardboard tubes, boxes, plastic balls, wooden blocks and whatever else you have on hand! Please ensure that any materials used are non-toxic and BPA free. Rabbits have teeth that grow continuously, so if you don't give them chew toys to keep their teeth filed down they may become overgrown which can lead to health problems. Clean branches and pieces of wood are good options as chew toys for rabbits but make sure they are non-toxic or not poisonous. Check with your breeder or veterinarian for guidance if necessary.

d.) Flemish Giant Rabbits Outdoors

Keeping domestic rabbits in outdoor cages (called hutches) is a fairly common practice. In most cases, domestic rabbits can cope with cold weather as long as they are provided adequate housing and shelter from wind, rain and snow. The Flemish Giant Rabbit is no exception to this rule – they are able to tolerate cold weather as long as they are properly protected.

One thing to be wary about with Flemish Giants in comparison to other domestic breeds is that they do not tend to do well in hot weather. Flemish Giant Rabbits are more likely to overheat than smaller breeds, so you must take extra precautions to ensure that they stay cool in the summer. One of the easiest ways to keep your rabbit cool is to freeze a 2-liter bottle of water and put it in your rabbit's cage so he can lean against it to cool down. You should also keep your Flemish Giant's cage out of direct sunlight so it doesn't get too warm.

As an alternative to keeping your rabbit outside permanently, you can also consider giving your rabbit an outdoor run or pen. This allows your rabbit to spend some time outside only when the weather and temperature is appropriate. A protected open exercise pen or rabbit run can be as large as you like but the walls should be high enough so your bunny can't jump over it.

If you choose to build an outdoor rabbit run, be sure to bury the wire at least a few inches/centimeters underground to prevent him from digging under it. Please also make sure the top of the pen is covered with for example, wire mesh so that predators cannot get in to attack your rabbit.

It is always recommended that you cover a large area of the pen with a towel or another solid object to provide your rabbit with shade. As always, make sure your rabbit has access to fresh water so he does not become dehydrated.

2.) Feeding Flemish Giant Rabbits

Given the size of the Flemish Giant Rabbit, you can probably already guess that it requires a lot more food than the average domestic rabbit. Not only is it important to provide your rabbit with enough food, however – you also have to offer the right kind of food. The type of diet you offer your rabbit will have a significant impact on his overall health and well-being. In this section you will learn the basics about your rabbit's nutritional needs as well as tips for feeding the right food in the right proportions.

a.) Nutritional Needs

Like all living things, Flemish Giant Rabbits require a balance of protein, carbohydrates and fat in their diet. Unlike predators, however, rabbits get their daily dose of protein and other nutrients from other sources – namely, hay. Some types of hay are higher in protein than others, so you need to be careful about what you offer your rabbit.

Young rabbits have higher needs for protein then adults so you should offer your baby bunnies protein-rich hay like alfalfa. Adult rabbits, however, should be offered hay with higher fiber content and lower protein content – hays should be a mixture of Alfalfa, Orchard and Timothy grass. However, be careful how you store your hay as you need to avoid mold growing on it as it can lead to illness.

Though offering plenty of hay is important for your rabbit's diet, perhaps the most essential element is a high-quality pellet feed. Rabbit pellets are commercially produced pellets designed to meet your rabbit's basic nutritional needs. It is important that you take the time to review the ingredients list on the package to determine whether it is a good quality food to offer your rabbit. If you purchase a low-quality feed, you may be purchasing a product that consists mainly of feed dust or one that contains artificial "binders". You should also be sure that the feed is free from corn and growth hormones. The main ingredient in your rabbit's pellets should be alfalfa – if it is first on the ingredients list that means it is the main ingredient by concentration.

When purchasing a pellet feed, look for formulas that contain at least 15 to 17% protein. With Flemish Giant rabbits in particular, it is a good idea to lean toward 17%

protein since their large bodies require more protein to support healthy growth and weight maintenance.

b.) How Much to Feed

The amount you feed your Flemish Giant will depend on its age and size. Younger rabbits should be fed as much hay and pellets as they will eat in order to support their growth. Once the rabbits mature however, at around 1 to 1.5 years of age, you should then begin limiting their intake of pellet food. An adult rabbit should receive about ½ cup (115 g) of pellets per 5 lbs. (2.26 kg) of body weight per day. Using this example, a 15 lbs. (6.80 kg) rabbit would receive about 1 ½ cups (345 g) of pellet food on a daily basis. Hay, on the other hand, is given freely as the rabbit wishes.

It is up to you how you choose to feed your rabbit, but many Flemish Giant owners choose to offer their rabbit's feed in multiple portions. For example, you might choose to feed your rabbit half of its daily pellet ration in the morning and the other half in the evening.

As already been mentioned, hay should be available at all times because your rabbit will eat it throughout the day. If you offer your rabbit fresh vegetables or fruits, do not offer them in large quantities because offering rabbits too much can be detrimental, especially to young rabbits whose stomachs are still sensitive. Approach these items as treats.

Treats high in carbohydrates should be avoided as rabbits have a tendency towards obesity. Food contaminated with chemicals should never be fed to rabbits.

Vegetables and Fruit Flemish Giants Enjoy:

Basil	Dandelion Greens
Bok Choy	Dill
Broccoli (leaves only)	Kale
Carrot	Mint
Celery	Mustard Greens
Cilantro	Parsley
Clover	Watercress
Collard Greens	

It is recommended that you don't feed lettuce and that cauliflower, broccoli and cabbage be avoided, as they cause gas and can lead to gastrointestinal stasis, which can be fatal.

Types of Fruits suitable for Flemish Giants:

Apples (fruit only)	Melon
Bananas	Papaya
Strawberries	Pears
Raspberries	Peaches
Pineapple	Blueberries

Don't be tempted to give too many treats. Vegetables and Fruits that that generate gas such be avoided as obesity will severely shorten your rabbits' lifespan.

c.) Poisonous Plants and Vegetables

There are certain foods and plants which can be very harmful for your Flemish Giant Rabbit. Before you feed your rabbit anything besides Alfalfa, Orchard and Timothy grass or pellets, check this list of foods:

Plants Harmful to Rabbits:

Acorns	Geranium
Aloe	Gladiola
Apple Seeds	Hemlock
Almonds	Hyacinth Bulbs
Asparagus Fern	Impatiens
Azalea	Iris
Carnations	Ivy
Clematis	Jasmine
Daffodil Bulbs	Jessamine
Eucalyptus	Juniper
Fruit Pits	Jack-in-the-Pulpit
Fruit Seeds	Laurel Lupine

Lily of the Valley	Philodendron
Marigold	Poinsettia
Milkweed	Rhubarb Leaves
Mistletoe	Sweet Potato
Nutmeg	Tansy
Oak	Tomato Leaves
Parsnip	Tulip Bulbs
Poppy	Violet
Peony	Yew

*This list is not comprehensive; in order to determine whether a specific plant is toxic for rabbits, consult the House Rabbit Society website:

http://rabbit.org/poisonous-plants

Commercial treats containing nuts, seeds, and grains should be avoided as they are not normal parts of the rabbit diet and provide unhealthy amounts of protein and starch and can lead to gastrointestinal stasis.

Your Flemish Giant will also require a continuous supply of clean fresh water usually provided for in a water crock, tip-proof ceramic pet dish, or hanging water bottle. It can be supplied using automatic systems or by manually providing feed and/or water as needed.

3.) Handling Flemish Giant Rabbits

Flemish Giant Rabbits make wonderful pets for a variety of reasons. Not only are they beautiful creatures and relatively easy to care for, but they are also very docile and tolerant to handling. One thing you need to be careful with in regard to Flemish Giants in particular is, of course, their size – do not attempt to handle a Flemish Giant unless you can do so safely. It is also important to remember that your rabbit can become frightened if handled roughly and they can inflict serious scratches with their powerful hind legs and sharp claws if they feel the need to struggle. This being the case, it is essential that you learn how to handle your rabbit properly.

If you want your rabbit to remain docile and friendly with humans, you need to handle him often. In order to do, that, however, you need to learn the proper method. Remember to exercise caution with children, as you do not want them attempting to pick up the rabbit unless they can support its weight fully.

When holding your rabbit, keep its feet facing down toward the ground and ensure that its spine is straight. Start by supporting his upper body with one arm around the chest and front legs and then wrap your other arm around the lower half making sure you support the rear legs. Gently but firmly hold the rabbit to your chest making sure you don't squeeze him or he may get frightened and struggle. Through the whole process, talk to him in a quiet and calm voice so that he is reassured that all is well. If he is not happy, then lower him to the ground as soon as possible.

Some Flemish Giant Rabbits can be "hypnotized" by laying them on their backs and rubbing their stomachs, but use caution when performing this trick to avoid injuring your rabbit.

a.) Steps to Handling Your Rabbit:

1. Remember never to pick your rabbit up by his ears, legs or tail.

2. Approach your rabbit slowly and bring yourself down to eye level – stroking his back may also help keep him calm.

3. Place your hand under the rabbit's torso and scoop him up, pulling him in close to your body.

4. Support the rabbit's hindquarters and hold him firmly against your body so he feels secure.

5. When you're ready to put your rabbit down, squat down and let him go carefully onto the ground or into his cage.

**Note: Do not be worried if your rabbit thumps you slightly with his legs as you release him – he is simply eager to get all four feet back on the ground where he feels most comfortable.

4.) Litter Training

If you have never owned a pet rabbit before, you may be surprised to hear that they can actually be litter trained. Rabbits are creatures of habit by nature, so you simply need to take advantage of this fact in order to train your rabbit to use a litter box. It may take a few weeks for your rabbit to begin using the litter box regularly, but it will definitely be worth the effort.

a.) Steps to Litter Training

1. Prepare a litter box using a plastic tub and compressed paper litter – you should also add some fresh hay so your rabbit can munch while using the litter box.

2. Scoop some feces from the cage into the litter box so your rabbit understands what it is to be used for – you can also add a urine-soaked paper towel to add to the scent.

3. Place a small treat like a few sprigs of fresh herbs in the litter box to entice your rabbit to use it.

4.   Find the area of the cage where your rabbit tends to prefer to do his business and place the litter box in that area – you may also start with several litter boxes and remove them as you find your rabbit's favorite.

5.   Limit your rabbit's freedom during training to ensure that he has to use the litter box to do his business.

6.   Clean up any accidents as quickly as possible and, if you catch your rabbit in the act of eliminating outside the litter box, move him to the litter box if you can!

7.   Gradually give your rabbit more space in the pen as he gets used to using the litter box – do not open it up too quickly or he may revert back to old habits.

5.) Other Care Tips

In addition to providing your Flemish Giant Rabbit with a clean habitat and a healthy diet, you should also keep an eye on his physical condition.

On the following pages I've listed some tips for keeping your Flemish Giant's ears, eyes, coat and teeth healthy as well as some common sense approach to electrical cords.

a.) Flemish Giant Ear Care

As is to be expected with their large size, a Flemish Giant's ears are very large as well. Just because they are large, however, doesn't necessarily mean they are more prone to infection than the ears of smaller breeds. Regardless what type of rabbit you own you should still perform regular checks on your rabbit's ears. Take a look inside your rabbit's ears for signs of wax buildup or infection at least once a week – unpleasant odor may also be a sign of infection.

Another sign you should keep an eye out for, particularly with Flemish Giants, is ears that start to flop over or bend. A Flemish Giant's ears should be naturally erect, standing a minimum of 5.25 inches (13.3 cm) tall (ARBA Standard). If your giant's ears begin to flop over, it could be because his cage is not tall enough – this is a fairly common problem. Ideally, your giant's cage should be at least 24 inches (61 cm).

b.) Skin and Coat Care

Your rabbit's feet should be dry and free from sores. If you notice patches of skin where the fur has worn away or swelling, you should seek immediate veterinary care. When petting your rabbit, take the time to check its skin and coat. If you notice white flakes or tiny white dots, your rabbit could have mites or fleas. Your veterinarian will be able to help you with a firm diagnosis and will also be able to recommend the proper treatment.

In addition to checking the condition of your rabbit's skin and coat, you should also plan to groom your rabbit regularly. Because they are so large, Flemish Giant Rabbits often have a more difficult time grooming themselves than smaller breeds – they can't always reach all parts of their bodies like smaller rabbits can. This being the case, you should go over your giant's coat with a slicker brush several times a week to remove dead hair and to keep his coat smooth and healthy.

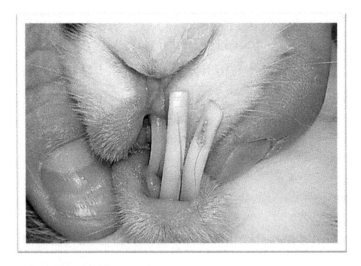

In some rabbits, the teeth are not properly aligned,
a condition called malocclusion.

c.) Flemish Giant Teeth Care

If you provide your rabbit with adequate chew toys, you shouldn't have to worry about its teeth becoming overgrown. You should, however, make frequent checks to see if the teeth are properly aligned – if they aren't, your rabbit could develop molar spurs or abscesses in the mouth and develop a condition called malocclusion. There are three main causes of this, the most common being genetic predisposition, injury or bacterial infection. If your rabbit's teeth become overgrown, you may have to take him to the veterinarian to have them trimmed.

d.) Trimming a Flemish Giant's Nails

The nails of Flemish Giant Rabbits grow continuously so you will need to trim them every six to eight weeks. Trimming your rabbit's nails is not a difficult task but it does require a degree of caution. Inside your rabbit's nail lies the quick – a vein which supplies blood to the nail. If you cut your rabbit's nails too short, you could sever the quick and induce severe bleeding. When clipping your rabbit's nails it is best to only cut off the pointed tip. To be safe, have your veterinarian show you how to properly trim a rabbit's nails before you try it yourself.

When trimming your Flemish Giant's nails, you have to remember that his legs are very powerful – more powerful than those of a smaller breed. For safety, you may want to have a friend or family member hold your rabbit to make sure he doesn't kick while you trim his nails. After a few times, your rabbit should start to get used to the process and he will hopefully start to calm down, letting you trim his nails without too much fuss.

e.) Eye Care

One of the most common causes of runny eyes in rabbits is a bacterial eye infection. These infections can be very dangerous and must be treated by a veterinarian as soon as possible. In many cases, antibiotics will be prescribed to handle the infection.

Obstructions and inflammation in the eye may be the result of natural or unnatural causes. In some cases, a piece of bedding or some other object may get stuck in the eye causing it to water or become inflamed. It is also possible, however, for a misshapen eyelid or part of the bone in the rabbit's face to cause an obstruction. If the flow of tears is obstructed, they may form a path down the cheek, discoloring the fur. Depending on the cause of the obstruction, surgery may be necessary to correct the issue.

If the rabbit's eyes do not produce enough tears on their own, they may become dry and irritated. When the eyes become too dry, they are more prone to scratches and erosions which can have a devastating effect on your rabbit's ability to see properly. Some of the symptoms of dry eyes include squinting, eye discharge, redness and inflammation. Trauma to the eye can also interfere with the production of tears and should be evaluated by a veterinarian. Depending what type of litter you use in your rabbit's cage, your rabbit could develop watery eyes as a result of allergies. Dust from the litter, hay or food in your rabbit's cage can get into the eyes and cause irritation. To prevent this from happening, choose litter that is dust-free and make sure the cage is well ventilated.

f.) Electrical Cords

Rabbits have a reputation for chewing on anything and they love electrical cords. To avoid any tragic results and any damage to your stereo, television, computer or telephone cable, there are some simple measures that can be taken with the obvious one being keeping cords out of their reach. Tack them to the wall or behind furniture or if necessary use a tough plastic tubing large enough for however many cords need protection, which if slit along the side can then be slipped over the cords. If all else fails, I saw a suggestion to rub some Tabasco sauce or bitter apple (indoor/outdoor repellent made for cats and dogs) on the cord. A bit of a messy solution but if the rabbit tries to chew and gets that bitter taste, it just might cure him. However, there is no guarantee that this will work.

Chapter Six: Health Issues

** **Note:** This section may be upsetting to any children who
may read it. Sadly like all our pets, Flemish Giant Rabbits
are susceptible to developing certain health issues.

O nce you bring your Flemish Giant home, he
becomes your responsibility. This being the case,
you need to provide your pet with the best possible
care to prevent him from becoming sick. No matter how
careful you are, however, rabbits are prone to developing
certain diseases.

In this chapter, I've given some details on the conditions to which the Flemish Giant breed is prone – with some guidance on diagnosing and treating them. Additionally, I've added some common sense precautions to take in helping to prevent disease in the first place.

1.) Common Health Problems

Note: Though some health conditions affecting Flemish Giant Rabbits can be treated at home, severe cases should always be examined by a veterinarian. If the disease is impacting your rabbit's health or mobility, do not delay in taking it to the vet.

As is true of all pets, the better the care you provide for your Flemish Giant, the healthier he will be. Unfortunately, you can't completely prevent your rabbit from ever coming into contact with a disease or getting sick, but you can equip yourself with the knowledge you need to handle the situation. The most common health problems seen include:

- Colibacillosis
- Dental Problems
- Dermatophytosis
- Enterotoxemia
- Fleas/Mites
- Listeriosis

- Mastitis
- Myxomatosis
- Otitis Media
- Papillomatosis
- Pasteurella
- Parasites

- Pneumonia
- Rhinitis
- Sore Hocks
- Uterine Cancer

- Viral Hemorrhagic Disease
- Wool Block

Colibacillosis

Colibacillosis is characterized by severe diarrhea and it is often caused by *Escherichia coli*. This disease can be seen in two forms depending on the rabbit's age. Newborn rabbits may exhibit a yellowish diarrhea – in newborns, this condition is often fatal and can affect the entire litter. In weaned rabbits, the intestines may fill with fluid and hemorrhages may surface.

In the case of weaned rabbits, the disease is typically fatal within 2 weeks. If the rabbit survives, it is likely to be stunted. Treatment is not often successful but, in mild cases, antibiotics may help. Rabbits that are severely affected with this disease should be culled to avoid the spread of the disease.

For Flemish Giant Rabbits in particular, diarrhea can also be caused by feeding too many vegetables. These rabbits have fairly sensitive stomachs and making sudden changes to their dietary routine can lead to gastrointestinal stress. If your Flemish Giant is suffering from diarrhea, however, you should not assume that is merely a problem with his diet – have him checked by a veterinarian.

Causes: *Escherichia coli*

Symptoms: yellowish diarrhea in newborns; fluid-filled intestines and hemorrhages in weaned rabbits

Treatment: antibiotics; treatment is not often effective

Dental Problems

All rabbits, including Flemish Giant Rabbits, are prone to developing dental problems. Though they may be larger than other domestic breeds, Flemish Giants have identical anatomy and thus no unique problems in regard to their teeth. The most common dental issues seen in domestic rabbits are overgrown molars and enamel spurs. Your rabbit's teeth may become overgrown or develop spurs if you don't provide enough fiber-rich foods. Fibrous foods are naturally abrasive which helps to keep your rabbit's teeth filed down. In most cases, dental problems require veterinary treatment so you should do your best to prevent them from happening in the first place.

Causes: diet too low in fiber

Symptoms: overgrown molars, enamel spurs

Treatment: veterinary exam and treatment

Dermatophytosis

Also known as ringworm, dermatophytosis is caused by either *Trichophyton mentagrophytes* or *Microsporum canis*. These infections typically result from poor husbandry or inadequate nutrition. Ringworm can be transmitted through direct contact with an infected rabbit or sharing tools such as brushes. The symptoms of ringworm include circular raised bumps on the body. The skin is these areas may be red and capped with a white, flaky material. Some of the most common treatments for ringworm include topical antifungal creams that contain miconazole or itraconazole. An effective solution is dipping your pet in a solution of water and 1% copper sulfate and carefully sponging his head.

Though all rabbits can be affected by ringworm, Flemish Giants that are kept in too small a cage are particularly at risk. If your giant isn't given a large enough cage, he could not only become stressed but he will also be living in his own filth, to some degree – this is not a healthy condition for your rabbit to be kept in. Flemish Giant rabbits are also at a higher risk for nutritional problems than smaller breeds because they require so much more food and thus, more nutrients. An improper diet can lead to many problems, including dermatophytosis.

Causes: *Trichophyton mentagrophytes* or *Microsporum canis*; typically results from poor husbandry or inadequate nutrition

Symptoms: circular raised bumps on the body; skin is red and capped with a white, flaky material

Treatment: include topical antifungal creams that contain miconazole or itraconazole; 1% copper sulfate dip

Enterotoxemia

Enterotoxemia is a disease characterized by explosive diarrhea and it typically affects rabbits between the ages of 4 and 8 weeks. Symptoms of this condition include lethargy, loss of condition and greenish-brown fecal matter around the perianal area. In many cases, this condition is fatal within 48 hours.

The primary cause of this disease is *Clostridium spiroforme*. These organisms are common in rabbits in small numbers but they can become a problem when the rabbit's diet is too low in fiber. Treatment may not be effective due to the rapid progression of the disease but adding cholestryamine or copper sulfate to the diet can help prevent enterotoxemia. Reducing stress in young rabbits and increasing fiber intake can also help.

Because Flemish Giant rabbits are so much larger than other domestic breeds, it makes sense that they require more food. You have to be careful, however, how you make up the difference. Do not overload your giant's diet with fresh vegetables because that could lead to more problems with diarrhea. Rather, make sure your rabbit gets plenty of fiber-rich hay and high-quality pellets to reduce his risk of gastrointestinal problems like enterotoxemia.

Causes: *Clostridium spiroforme*

Symptoms: lethargy, loss of condition and greenish-brown fecal matter around the perianal area

Treatment: may not be effective; adding cholestryamine or copper sulfate to the diet can help prevent

Fleas/Mites

Indoor rabbits are unlikely to contract fleas and ticks on their own unless you have a dog or cat. If your rabbit spends time outside or if you have other pets that spend time outside, however, your rabbit could be at risk. Mites are typically found in the ears and fur of rabbits and they most often present themselves after your rabbit's immune system has already been compromised. This could happen if you feed your Flemish Giant an inadequate diet or if he is stressed from being kept in a cage that is too small.

Fur mites tend to stay at the base of the neck or near the rabbit's rear. If left untreated, mites and fleas can cause severe itching, bald spots and bleeding. The best treatment for fleas and mites is a prescription medication called Revolution, known in the UK as Stronghold. Another treatment option in the UK is Ivermectin drops. Flea and mite infestations are particularly difficult to treat with Flemish Giant rabbits because these rabbits have so much more area to cover. Even a few fleas or mites can quickly reproduce to cause a big problem, so don't take any chances with your Flemish Giant!

Causes: exposure to infested pets, spending time outside

Symptoms: itching, bald spots, bleeding

Treatment: prescription medication; Revolution in the US, Stronghold or Ivermectin in the UK

Listeriosis

Listeriosis is a type of sporadic septicemia which often causes sudden death or abortion – this condition is most common in pregnant Does. Some of the contributing factors for this disease include poor husbandry and stress. Some of the common symptoms include anorexia, depression and weight loss. If you intend to breed your Flemish Giants, make sure you give the Doe plenty of space and keep the cage clean and sanitary. Prevention is the best way to deal with this disease.

Even if you take precautions, however, your Flemish Giant could still be affected by listeriosis. If not properly treated, the *Listeria monocytogenes* responsible for the disease can spread to the blood, liver and uterus. Treatment is not often attempted because diagnosis is not frequently made premortem.

Causes: *Listeria monocytogenes*

Symptoms: anorexia, depression and weight loss; often causes sudden death or abortion

Treatment: not often attempted because diagnosis is not frequently made premortem

Mastitis

This condition is most commonly seen in rabbitries but it can affect single rabbits. Mastitis is a condition that affects pregnant Does and it is caused by *staphylococci bacteria*. The bacteria infect the mammary glands, causing them to become hot, red and swollen. If the disease is allowed to progress, it may cause septicemia and become fatal. If you plan to breed your Flemish Giant Does, this is one condition you definitely need to take precautions against.

Does affected by mastitis are unlikely to eat but they will crave water. The rabbit may also run a fever. Treatment for this condition may include antibiotic treatment. Penicillin, however, should be avoided because it can cause diarrhea. Kits should not be fostered because they will only end up spreading the disease.

Causes: *staphylococci bacteria*

Symptoms: hot, red and swollen mammary glands; loss of appetite; fever

Treatment: antibiotics

Myxomatosis

Myxomatosis is a viral disease that is caused by *myxoma virus*. This condition is typically fatal and it can be transmitted through direct contact or through biting insects. Some of the initial symptoms of the disease include conjunctivitis, eye discharge, listlessness, anorexia and fever. In severe cases, death may occur after only 48 hours.

Treatment for this condition is generally not effective and it can cause severe and lasting damage. There is however, a vaccine available against myxomatosis. This vaccine should be given after the rabbit reaches 6 weeks of age.

Causes: by *myxoma virus*; transmitted through direct contact or through biting insects

Symptoms: conjunctivitis, eye discharge, listlessness, anorexia and fever

Treatment: generally not effective; vaccine is available

Otitis Media

Also called "wry neck" or "head tilt," otitis media is caused by an infection resulting from *P multocida* or *Encephalitozoon cunuculi*. These bacteria cause the accumulation of fluid or pus in the ear, causing the rabbit to tilt its head. Antibiotic therapy may be effective, though it may just worsen the condition. In most cases, rabbits infected with this condition are culled.

This condition is of particular concern for Flemish Giant Rabbits because their ears are so large. The size of the ears doesn't necessarily make these rabbits more prone to infection, but it does increase the risk for exposure to bacteria which could lead to infection if you don't care for your rabbit's ears properly. You should examine your rabbit's ears often for signs of infection and do everything you can to keep them clean.

Causes: *P multocida* or *Encephalitozoon cunuculi* bacteria

Symptoms: accumulation of fluid or pus in the ear, causing the rabbit to tilt its head

Treatment: antibiotic therapy may be effective

Papillomatosis

Papillomatosis is fairly common in domestic rabbits and it is caused by the *rabbit oral papillomavirus*. This disease results in the formation of small grey nodules or warts on the underside of the tongue or floor of the mouth. Another type, caused by cottontail papillomavirus, may produce horned warts on the neck, shoulders, ears and abdomen. There is no treatment for these conditions but the lesions typically go away on their own in time.

Causes: rabbit oral papillomavirus

Symptoms: small grey nodules or warts on the underside of the tongue or floor of the mouth

Treatment: no treatment; the lesions typically go away on their own in time

Parasites

One of the most common parasites found in Flemish Giant Rabbits is *Encephalitozoon cuniculi*. This protozoan parasite can survive in the body for years without causing any harm. In some cases, however, the parasite can cause severe damage. This parasite typically causes nerve damage which results in head tilting, incontinence, paralysis and rupture of the lens of the eye.

Intestinal worms are also a common problem in rabbits. Both of these conditions can be treated with de-worming paste. This treatment can be used for infected rabbits and as a preventive against parasites. When used as a preventive, the paste is typically administered twice a year.

Causes: *Encephalitozoon cuniculi*, intestinal worms

Symptoms: head tilting, incontinence, paralysis and rupture of the lens of the eye

Treatment: de-worming paste

Pasteurella

This condition is a respiratory disease caused by the *Pasteurella mulctocida* bacteria which has several strains – some of which have been known to cause pneumonia. Pasteurella is often referred to as "snuffles" because it causes nasal discharge as well as sneezing and congestion. If the rabbit wipes its nose with its paws, the fur on the paws and legs may become matted.

Unfortunately there is no vaccine for pasteurella, though it can often be treated with antibiotics. Depending on the severity of the case, treatment may be continued for weeks or months before symptoms abate. Even if the rabbit's condition improves on antibiotics, the symptoms may return after the treatment is stopped. If the rabbit recovers, it can still become a carrier and spread the disease to others.

Causes: *Pasteurella multocida bacteria*

Symptoms: nasal discharge, sneezing and congestion

Treatment: antibiotic treatment often used, may be necessary to treat for several weeks or months

Pneumonia

Pneumonia is fairly common in domestic rabbits and it is most often a secondary infection. The most common cause of pneumonia in rabbits is *P multocida* bacteria, though other kinds may be involved. A precursor of pneumonia is often upper respiratory disease which may be a result of inadequate ventilation or sanitation.

Some of the common symptoms of pneumonia include listlessness, fever and anorexia. Once they show symptoms, most rabbits succumb to the infection within 1 week. Though antibiotic treatment is often used, it is not typically effective because it may not be administered until the disease is highly advanced.

Causes: *P multocida bacteria*

Symptoms: listlessness, fever and anorexia

Treatment: antibiotic treatment is often used but not typically effective

Rhinitis Sinusitis

Rhinitis is the medical term used to describe sniffling or chronic inflammation in the airway and lungs. This condition is often caused by *Pastuerella* which has historically been quoted as the primary respiratory disease of rabbits, which manifests itself most commonly as Rhinitis, though *Staphylococcus* or *Streptococcus* may also be involved. The initial symptom of this disease is a thin stream of mucus flowing from the nose. As the disease progresses, the flow may encrust the fur on the paws and chest. Sneezing and coughing may also be exhibited. This condition generally resolves itself but even recovered rabbits can be carriers of the disease.

Causes: is often caused by *Pastuerella*, though *Staphylococcus* or *Streptococcus* may also be involved

Symptoms: sniffling or chronic inflammation in the airway and lungs; thin stream of mucus flowing from the nose

Treatment: generally resolves itself

Sore Hocks

Sore hocks is a condition to which Flemish Giant Rabbits are particularly prone. In many cases, it results from the rabbit being kept in a cage with a wire floor that causes abrasions to the feet, allowing for the spread of infection. This is a condition in which the fur on the legs or feet begins to wear away. As the fur is worn away, skin or even bone may be exposed and sores or abscesses may result. This condition typically affects the hind legs and feet, though it can be seen in the front feet as well.

Causes: wire cage bottom, no solid place to rest

Symptoms: fur wearing away, exposed skin or bone, sores or abscesses

Treatment: treatment of sores and abscesses, installing solid cage bottom, proper sanitation

Uterine Cancer

A common cause of death in female rabbits, uterine cancer can easily be prevented. Spaying female rabbits between the ages of 5 months and 2 years is the best way to prevent this disease. In un-spayed female rabbits, uterine cancer can spread to several different organs before the disease is diagnosed. At that point, treatment is typically ineffective.

Causes: tumor growing in the uterus

Symptoms: other reproductive issues; endometriosis, bulging veins, vaginal discharge, bloody urine

Treatment: spaying female rabbits to prevent; once the cancer develops, treatment is generally ineffective

Viral Hemorrhagic Disease

Also called rabbit hemorrhagic disease, viral hemorrhagic disease is transmitted through direct contact or contaminated food, water and bedding. Unfortunately, there is no effective treatment for this condition and many rabbits die from it without ever showing symptoms. Some of the most common symptoms of viral hemorrhagic disease include difficulty breathing, paralysis, lethargy, bloody discharge from the nose, weight loss and convulsions. Once symptoms appear, the disease is typically fatal within 2 weeks.

Causes: rabbit calcivirus; transmitted through direct contact or contaminated food, water and bedding

Symptoms: difficulty breathing, paralysis, lethargy, bloody discharge from the nose, weight loss and convulsions

Treatment: no effective treatment

Wool Block

All breeds are prone to developing a dangerous condition called Wool Block although it is most prevalent in wooly breeds. Wool Block occurs when a ball of hair forms in the stomach and intestines of the rabbit, preventing it from digesting any food. This can lead to inadequate nutrition and eventual starvation and death. Rabbits are incapable of vomiting to clear the hairball.

It is recommended that you speak to your breeder before purchasing your rabbit as some people feel that a pre-disposition to wool block can be inherited. You can check with your breeder whether it is a problem that they have experienced with their stock. There are several things that you can do to help prevent and diagnose wool block. Your rabbit must have access to fresh de-chlorinated water at all times and should have lots of exercise. It is essential that your rabbit is fed with a diet that is high in fiber and contains plenty of hay.

Many owners supplement with papaya tablets or fresh papaya or pineapple chunks once a week as the enzymes in these help dissolve the food within the fiber and therefore allow it to be passed more easily through the intestines. Other owners will on one day each week feed their rabbit hay and two tablespoons of whole oats and/or extra fresh vegetables. On this day, they do not feed their rabbit any pellets, allowing their stomach an opportunity to clean out. You should also ensure that your rabbit is groomed properly to reduce the amount of hair that they ingest.

Additionally you should study their droppings each day and become familiar with what is normal for your rabbit and note any changes. Droppings that become smaller or are a string of beads mixed with hair can be a sign of wool block. Due to the seriousness of this condition, if you are in any doubt, you should seek veterinarian advice immediately.

Causes: Ball of hair in the stomach and intestines

Symptoms: Changes in eating patterns, weight loss, change in droppings, lethargy

Treatment: Seek veterinarian attention as opinions vary on treatment

2.) Preventing Illness

While you cannot completely prevent your Flemish Giant from ever coming into contact with disease, you can take precautions to keep him safe and healthy. There are several things you can do to help protect your rabbit against disease -- the most important thing, however, is to provide your rabbit with a clean, healthy environment. It is essential that you clean your rabbit's cage on a regular basis and provide plenty of fresh water, de-chlorinated if possible, for him to drink. You should also think carefully about your rabbit's diet and make sure to keep him up to date on any vaccinations he might need.

a.) Dangerous/Toxic Foods

There are certain foods and plants which can be very harmful for your Flemish Giant Rabbit. Please refer to the list of foods that can cause serious problems in the Feeding section in Chapter Five. You can also check with your vet or local breeder on any local foodstuffs that you might consider feeding your rabbit to help prevent unnecessary health problems.

b.) Recommended Vaccinations

Depending where in the world you live, having your rabbit vaccinated is one of the best things you can do to protect him from disease. Two of the most important vaccines for domestic rabbits are against myxomatosis and viral hemorrhagic disease (VHD) – both of these vaccinations are highly recommended in the U.K. These vaccines are available as single vaccines, which need to be taken nine days apart every six months, or as a single combined vaccine once a year.

After you bring your rabbit home, it is a sensible precaution to have it examined by a vet as soon as possible. Your vet will be able to assess your rabbit's condition and set a schedule for future check-ups. Additionally, your vet will also offer recommendations on what vaccines your rabbit needs and how often he needs them. It may seem like a needless cost to take your rabbit to the vet once a year but it can save you a lot of money and heartache in diagnosing serious diseases before they become untreatable.

Note: Some rabbit owners believe that vaccinations are not necessary in order for a rabbit to remain healthy. Ultimately, it is your decision whether you choose to vaccinate your rabbit or not. Before you make a decision, consult your veterinarian.

3.) Pet Insurance Pros and Cons

Many pet owners have discovered that pet insurance helps defray the costs of veterinary expenses. Pet insurance is similar to health insurance in that you pay a monthly premium and a deductible (excess in the UK) and the pet insurance pays for whatever is covered in your plan and can include annual exams and blood work. Shopping for pet insurance is similar to shopping for health insurance in the United States. As with health insurance, the age and the overall health of your rabbit will determine how much you will pay in premiums and deductibles. Ask plenty of questions to determine the best company and plan for your needs. Some of the questions that you should ask are:

- Can you go to your regular vet, or do you have to go to a vet assigned by the pet insurance company?

- What does the insurance plan cover? Does it cover annual exams? Surgeries? Emergency illness and injury?

- Does coverage begin immediately?

- Are pre-existing conditions covered? In addition, if your rabbit develops a health issue and you later have to renew the policy, is that condition covered when you renew your policy?

- Is medication covered?

- Do you have to have pre-authorization before your pet receives treatment? What happens if your rabbit has the treatment without pre-authorization?

- Is there a lifetime maximum benefit amount? If so, how much is that amount?

Take the time to research your pet insurance options. Compare the different plans available, what each covers, and the cost before making the decision on which is best for you and your pet.

Pet insurance may not be the answer for everyone. While pet insurance may not be a feasible option for you, consider having a backup plan, just in case your rabbit requires emergency care or you run into unexpected veterinarian costs.

A simple way to prepare for an emergency is to start a veterinary fund for your rabbit. Decide to put a certain amount of money aside each week, each month, or each paycheck to use in the case of an emergency. Think about the potential financial costs of veterinary care and plan for how you will pay for it now instead of waiting until something occurs.

Companies in the United States offering pet insurance include:

Healthy Paws

HealthyPawsPetInsurance.com

PetPlan

GoPetPlan.com

Embrace

EmbracePetInsurance.com

Trupanion

Trupanion.com

Pets Best

PetsBest.com

Pet Premium

Enroll.PetPremium.com

The ASPCA

ASPCAPetInsurance.com

PetInsurance

PetInsurance.com

Pet First

PetFirst.com

24PetWatch

24PetWatch.com

Pet insurance companies in the United Kingdom include:

DirectLine

Directline.com/pet-insurance

VetsMediCover

Vetsmedicover.co.uk

PetPlan

Petplan.co.uk

Churchill

Churchill.com/pet-insurance

Animal Friends

Animalfriends.org.uk

Healthy Pets

Healthy-pets.co.uk

For a comprehensive comparison of policies see:

Money.co.uk/pet-insurance.htm

Please note that all companies and links were valid at the time of publication in early 2014, but like all Internet content are subject to change. Since pet insurance is growing rapidly in popularity, use the search engine of your choice to look for additional coverage options. Note that the vast majority of sites allow visitors to obtain an estimate price quote online.

Chapter Seven: Breeding

You have probably heard the phrase "breeding like rabbits" tossed around. This phrase simply points to the fact that rabbits are prolific breeders and the Flemish Giant is no exception. These rabbits breed fairly easily and regularly with little to no effort required on the part of the owner.

If you want to breed your Flemish Giant, however, think carefully before doing so to ensure that you can provide your pregnant Doe and her kits with the care they require. In this chapter I've put together some of the basics about preparing your Flemish Giant for breeding as well as some tips for raising the kits once they are born. It is not designed as an exhaustive guide and if you think that you would like to breed your rabbit, I strongly recommend speaking to your breeder to obtain more in depth information.

1.) Basic Breeding Information

Before you try to breed your Flemish Giant Rabbits, you need to think about your motivation for doing so. If you are simply looking to make some money on selling the kits, think again – many rabbit breeders are lucky to come out even after veterinary costs and the expenses associated with raising the babies. If, however, you simply love the breed and want to improve or preserve the Flemish Giant, that is a better reason for breeding.

In addition to thinking about why you want to breed, there are some basic facts you should be aware of. One important piece of information is that male Flemish Giants reach sexual maturity fairly quickly – in many cases, they can become sexually mature by the time they reach the age of 5 months.

This information is important for a number of reasons. First, if you plan to raise baby rabbits you will need to separate the sexes before this point to prevent unwanted breeding. Second, you should not attempt to breed a rabbit before it reaches sexual maturity.

While male Flemish Giants may be capable of reproducing as early as 5 months, females may not be ready until around 8 or 9 months. Generally, you shouldn't breed a female Flemish Giant until she reaches a weight of 14 lbs. (6.35 kg) according to guidelines given by ARBA.

This would mean that you Doe would be typically be between 9 and 12 months old by this stage. There are varying opinions as to how often you then breed for and it is really a personal decision. Some breeders advocate not having any more litters after the age of three years while others feel comfortable continuing to produce quality litters for five to eight years.

A note of caution here in that as the Doe reaches a year old, her pelvic bones may begin to fuse. This will make it more challenging for her to deliver her kits, and a problematic delivery can mean death for her and her unborn kits. As the Doe gets older it may develop too much fat around the ovaries which could result in difficulty conceiving.

Experienced rabbit breeders will recommend that you always plan your litters – the gestational period of an Flemish Giant Rabbit is between 28 and 31 days so be sure to mark the day on your calendar. Before breeding, it is important to feed your rabbits a healthy diet so they are in good condition for breeding. If either rabbit is not in optimal condition, it is unlikely to have much interest in breeding – if breeding should occur it is then also less likely to be successful.

2.) The Breeding Process

The breeding process for Flemish Giant Rabbits does not require much effort on your part – all you have to do is bring the Doe to the Buck's cage when you determine that the pair is ready for breeding. It is best to bring the Doe to the Buck's cage because the Buck will be less distracted if he is in his own environment while Does are very defensive about their cage and may cause injury to the Buck if he enters her territory.

The best time to attempt breeding is in the morning. It is important that you do not leave the rabbits unattended during breeding for several reasons. First, you want to be sure that the act actually takes place. Second, you need to be around to separate the pair if one of the two becomes hostile or aggressive. After coupling the doe a minimum of three times the buck should be removed to his cage.

After introducing the pair, breeding should occur fairly quickly. Wait for the Buck to make a high-pitched squeal or grunt and to fall off the Doe – at this point, you should remove the Buck from the cage. How quickly you let them mate again is yet another personal choice. Some breeders advocate three successful mounts during this meeting and no further contact; others give a break of just one hour to ensure a successful mating, while others leave it until the following day to increase the chances of ovulation and a successful pregnancy. You won't be able to tell for sure that the Doe is pregnant until about 15 days later. Look for swollen nipples at this point and a hardened lower stomach area.

Up until your Doe reaches the halfway point in her pregnancy (about 15 days), continue to feed her normal rations. After this point, however, you should increase her rations by about 50% to provide fuel for milk production. After about 24 days you may be able to feel the babies moving around inside the Doe's belly – if you try to feel them, be very careful so you don't injure the mother or the babies.

About 5 days before your Doe's due date, place a nest box measuring about 20 by 20 by 24 inches (50.8 x 50.8 x 61 cm) in the cage. The size of your nest box requirements may vary depending on the size of your particular Doe. Some Does will begin to build a nest before this point, but you must still provide a nest box so the babies will be able to stay warm after they are born. Metal nest boxes are preferable to wooden ones because they can be easily disinfected and are less likely to harbor bacteria. Place the nest box in a corner of the cage away from the toilet area where your rabbit can access it easily. If you are using a metal box, remove the bottom and line it with 2 or 3 layers of cardboard then fill the bottom of the box with soft bedding that the Doe can arrange as she likes.

If you are worried about the temperature in your home, you might want to place a specialist low-wattage lamp about 12 inches (30.5 cm) over the box to keep your kits warm. Heat lamps with thermostats are available in a price range of $35 to $50 (£22.75 to £32.50) with replacement bulbs averaging $10 to $15 (£6.50 to £9.75). Ensure that you get a specialist heat lamp to reduce the risk of fire.

3.) Raising the Babies

The main thing you need to be concerned about with raising Flemish Giant kits is the space required. Whereas a cage for a single Flemish Giant should be about a minimum of 30 by 72 inches (76.2 by 182.9 cm), a cage for a pregnant Doe and her litter should be a minimum of 60-by-96 inches (152.4 by 243.8 cm). Included in this cage should also be a nest box measuring at least 20 by 20 by 24 inches (50.8 x 50.8 x 61 cm) As I have said before, these are the minimum sizes and I recommend as big as you can provide.

As the kits grow, they will start to take up more space physically, but they will also require a lot of space to move around. Considering the size of an average Flemish Giant litter contains 5 to 12 kits, you are going to need a significant amount of space to raise the babies.

Flemish Giant Does go through a gestation period lasting between 28 and 31 days. At the end of this period on day 30 to 32, they will give birth to a litter of kits – baby rabbits. The average litter size for Flemish Giant Rabbits is fairly large, generally between 5 and 12 kits but it can be up to 18 but then some won't receive as much milk as others so will be small and less developed when they reach maturity. Kits that fall behind in their growth before they are weaned typically never develop to their full potential.

As long as the Doe's first litter is born before she is 1 year old, the birthing process should go smoothly. After this point, however, the pelvic bones may become fused, making it harder for her to give birth. As I mentioned earlier, how long you breed is a personal choice and it will vary from one rabbit to another, but generally it is recommended that Does no longer be bred after they reach 3 years of age.

Try not to disturb the Doe when she is giving birth, which generally takes place the early morning hours and then wait for her to rest a little bit and to calm down. At this point you should carefully remove the nest box from the cage and open it somewhere safe to count the kits. Remove any afterbirth, soiled nesting material and stillborn kits. You should also take a minute to inspect the kits themselves to be sure there are no injuries or birth defects. Place the nesting material and the kits back into the nesting box and place it back in the cage.

Though Flemish Giant Rabbits require more food than other domestic breeds, you should be careful not to over feed your pregnant Does. While the Doe is nursing her young, you should continue to feed her the same amount of food she received before giving birth – continue this for a few days. After the first few days following the birth, however, you should slowly increase the amount of food until the pellets are available at all times so both the Doe and the kits have access to it. You should always keep fresh hay available in the cage as well. Not only will the Doe eat it but the kits may nibble on it as well as they grow older and their digestive systems begin to develop properly.

On a daily basis, it is suggested you check the nest to be sure none have died. At this time, the Doe can very protective and although she will know your scent and shouldn't complain, she may jump at you when you probe the nest. I'd recommend you pay her some attention, pet her and perhaps give her a treat to divert her attention before attempting to remove the box to check on the kits. By handling and touching the newborn kits from the start, you will make them gentler and easier to handle.

It generally takes about 10 to 12 days for Flemish Giant Rabbit kits to start to open their eyes. If they have not opened by day 12, use a damp cotton ball and gently wipe the eyelids from one corner to the other until the eyes open. It is not uncommon for the eyes to close again after opening, so simply repeat the process until the eyes stay open on their own. Be very careful when handling your Flemish Giant kits so you do not accidentally injure them.

By the time the kits reach about 3 to 3 ½ weeks of age they should be ready to live completely outside the nest box. Until that point you should clean the nest box every 3 to 4 days, removing soiled litter and old hay. When you have removed the box, you can place the nesting material in the same corner allowing the babies a secure section of the cage to sleep.

Once your kits reach 6 to 8 weeks of age, they are ready to be weaned. In many cases, they will naturally wean themselves by nursing less from their mother and accepting more solid food. If you need to wean the kits yourself, however, you can start by removing the largest 2 kits to a separate cage away from the others. After a few days, remove another pair to a separate cage and repeat the process as needed. By the time the kits are about 9 weeks of age you should separate the sexes.

Baby rabbits can be free-fed pellets and hay until they reach about 7 months of age. During this period they should be given access to plenty of fresh water. You can begin to introduce small amounts of fresh vegetables once the kits reach 12 weeks of age. When the kits reach 7 months of age, start to limit them to ½ cup (115 g) of pellets per 5 lbs. (2.27 kg) bodyweight. After 1 year of age, cut back again to only ¼ to ½ cup (57.5 to 115 g) of pellets a day per 6 lbs. (2.72 kg) bodyweight. At this point, you should also begin to incorporate at least 2 cups (150 g) of fresh veggies per day in your rabbit's diet.

When introducing vegetables into the diet for your kits it is important to do so carefully so you do not upset their stomachs. Start with small amounts of carrots, kale or romaine lettuce and then introduce one vegetable at a time – if your rabbit develops diarrhea, wait a little longer before trying again. Avoid iceberg lettuce and celery as these foods have very high water content with relatively little nutritional value for young rabbits.

Sexing Your Rabbit

It is challenging to tell the difference between a Buck and a Doe in young rabbits and will take some time and practice to learn. The following may be of some assistance.
1. Turn the rabbit over onto its back. 2. Using one hand take a hold of the scruff of the rabbit's neck and with the other hand hold the rabbit's tail between your index and middle fingers. Then softly press down just above the sexual cavity with your thumb until either a 'slit' or a 'circle' is spotted. The 'slit' profile indicates that the rabbit is a Doe while the 'circle' profile means it is a Buck.

As they grow older, this will get a lot easier with either the penis or the vagina being very obvious. However, in young rabbits this can be harder to spot as scent glands in a young female can be incorrectly identified for emerging testicles while males can also pull their testicles in to their abdomen. If you have any uncertainty or worries, then check with your Vet but even they are known to get it wrong.

Chapter Eight: Showing Flemish Giant Rabbits

F lemish Giant Rabbits continue to be one of the most
popular breeds for show. These rabbits are large,
beautiful creatures and showing your rabbit can be a
wonderful experience for the both of you.

Before you decide to show your Flemish Giant, however,
you should be sure that your rabbit meets the requirements
and that you are ready for the challenge. In this chapter I
will give you the basics about showing rabbits and
introduce you to the Flemish Giant breed standard as well.

1.) Breed Standard

Before you can show your Flemish Giant Rabbit you need to make sure that he will be accepted into the show in the first place. Only rabbits that meet the breed standard for any given breed will be accepted for show. A breed standard is simply the approved description of the breed published by the breed club – it dictates the acceptable appearance, size, color and condition of rabbits within the breed.

Below you will find explanations of the Flemish Giant Rabbit breed standard as set forth by the British Rabbit Council in the U.K. and the American Rabbit Breeders Association in the U.S.

a.) British Rabbit Council (BRC) Standard

Size and Weight – Bucks weighing no less than 11 lbs. (4.99kg) and Does no less than 12 lbs. (5.44kg); size is considered irrespective of weight

Body – Large and flat with a broad forehead and hindquarters; Does should have an evenly carried dewlap

Legs and Feet – Strong in bone, large and proportionate to body; feet are velvety and ticked

Head and Ears – Head is large and full; eyes are bold and dark brown; ears are held erect.

Coat and Condition – Full coat is short, firm and moderately thick

Color – dark steel grey with even or wavy ticking; fur until the belly and tail is white

Summary of Points:

Color: **30**

Size and Weight: **20**

Body: **15**

Legs and Feet: **15**

Head and Ears: **10**

Coat and Condition: **10**

Total: 100

b.) American Rabbit Breeders Association Standard

Body – The body is long and powerful with full, broad forequarters and hindquarters. Good muscular development, body arching from behind the shoulder blades to above the haunches. Does display a full dewlap.

Head, Ears and Eyes – Head is large and broad; Ears are erect with a heavy ear base; at least 6 inches (15 cm) tall. Eyes are dark and have a rueful expression.

Legs and Feet – Straight and large; proportional to body size; toenails are evenly colored.

Fur – Fur is glossy, full and dense. Coat rolls back to normal position. Color is blue when stroked from hindquarters to the shoulders.

Color – Uniform color in all varieties: black, blue, fawn, light gray, sandy, steel gray and white.

Summary of Points:

Body: **35**

Head: **6**

Ears: **4**

Eyes: **2**

Legs and Feet: **6**

Tail: **2**

Fur: **15**

Color: **20**

Condition: **10**

Total: 100

2.) What to Know Before Showing

There are a number of things you should know and do before deciding to take part in a show. The first thing you need to do is to familiarize yourself with all the relevant literature and guidance provided by the show society concerned. Satisfy yourself that your rabbit will meet their standards.

Flemish Giants are generally shown in three different classifications as recognition of the fact of how much slower they are to mature compared to other breeds. These are: -

1) Juniors. Rabbits up to 6 months.

2) Intermediate. Rabbits from 6 to 8 months.

3) Senior. All rabbits over 8 months with Does having a minimum weight requirement of 14 lbs. (6.35 kg) and Bucks a minimum of 13 lbs. (5.90 kg). (ARBA Standard).

In addition to the breakdown of points, you should keep in mind the faults and disqualifications for the Flemish Giant breed.

Faults/Disqualifications for Flemish Giant Rabbits:

- Body length under 20 inches (50.8 cm) on seniors
- Short, blocky body
- Ears with a thin, weak base

- Ear length under 5.25 inches (13.3 cm)

- Toenails not matching on the same foot

- Thin or very short coat; flying coat

- Smudgy or patchy color

- Dark ticking in sandy color

- Yellow case or stains in white rabbits

- Ring color over the back

- Coat any color other than those accepted

**Note: Faults may vary by competition so do your research before you submit your rabbit for show.

3.) Packing for a Show

The key to success in rabbit shows is to be prepared. This involves making sure your rabbit meets the breed standard and arranging the rabbit properly for judging. You should also prepare yourself by bringing along an emergency kit, just in case.

Included in your emergency kit should be:

- Nail clippers – for emergency nail trimming

- Antibiotic ointment

- Band-Aids – for minor injuries to self, not rabbit

- Hydrogen peroxide – for cleaning injuries and spots on white coats

- Slicker brush – to smooth rough coats

- Black felt-tip pen

- Business cards

- Paper towels – because you never know

- Scrap carpet square – for last-minute grooming

- Collapsible stool – when chairs are not available

- Extra clothes

- Supplies for your rabbits

Chapter Nine: Flemish Giant Rabbits Care Sheet

Keeping your Flemish Giant Rabbit healthy requires that you provide him with the best care possible. In order to do that, however, you need to learn everything you can about the breed.

In this chapter I've summarized all the important facts about keeping Flemish Giants Rabbits that you need to know. Rather than flipping through the entire book to find tidbits about the breed's size or breeding habits, check this care sheet!

1.) Basic Breed Information

Classification: pet breed

Origins: originated in Flanders, probably descendant from meat and fur rabbits (possibly the Patagonian)

Weight: 14 to 18 lbs. (6.35 to 8.16 kg) at maturity

Length: up to 32 inches (81.3 cm)

Height: 16 to 18 inches (40.6 to 45.7 cm)

Body Shape: long with broad hindquarters

Body Structure: powerful with good muscular development; females have a dewlap

Coat: dense and glossy, rolls back

Coat Color: black, blue, fawn, light grey, sandy, steel grey or white (accepted by ARBA)

Temperament: docile and tolerant of handling

Lifespan: average 5 to 7 years

Other Pets: gets along well with cats and dogs

2.) Housing Requirements

Minimum Cage Size: 30 by 72 inches (76.2 by 182.9 cm)

Breeding Cage Size: 60 by 96 inches (152.4 by 243.8 cm)

Minimum Cage Height: 24 inches (61 cm)

Location Options: indoor vs. outdoor

Indoor Location Tips: away from drafts, not in direct sunlight, away from heating/cooling vents

Cage Materials: galvanized welded wire, solid metal or plastic bottom

Bedding: non-toxic pellets, fresh hay, newspaper

Accessories: water bottle, food bowls, haywheel, litter pan, chew toys

3.) Diet and Nutritional Needs

Diet Basics: about 15 to 17% protein, high fiber

Main Diet: high-quality grass hay (Timothy Orchard and Alfalfa)

Commercial Pellets: about 17% protein

Supplemental Foods: fresh vegetable greens, fruits, seeds

Amount to Feed (juvenile): unlimited hay, unlimited pellets

Amount to Feed (adult): unlimited hay; 1/2 cup (115 g pellets) per 5 lbs. (2.27 kg) bodyweight; up to 2 cups (150 g) green vegetables daily

Other Needs: unlimited supply of fresh water

Treats: fresh fruit, carrots, sunflower seeds, kale, romaine lettuce

4.) Breeding Information

Sexual Maturity: 5 to 6 months of age for Bucks and 8 to 9 months for Does

Breeding Age: at least 9 months or 14 lbs. (6.35 kg) for females

Gestation Period: about 28 to 31 days

Signs of Pregnancy: swollen nipples and hardened belly (15 days)

Pregnant Diet: normal rations to day 15, then increase by 50% daily ration

Nest Box Materials: metal box is ideal, line bottom with cardboard and hay

Nest Box Dimensions: 20 by 20 by 24 inches (50.8 x 50.8 x 61 cm)

Insert Nest Box: about 5 days before due date

Average Litter Size: 5 to 12 kits

Eyes Open: 10 to 12 days after birth

Leave Nest Box: 3 to 3 1/2 weeks

Weaning Age: 6 to 8 weeks

Separate Sexes: 9 to 10 weeks to differentiate between the sexes

5.) Other Care Tips

Handling: support body, keep all legs facing floor

Litter Training: possible; can take several weeks

Health Check: check ears for wax build-up/infection; feet for sores; fur for mites and swelling; teeth for overgrowth/malocclusion

Grooming: easy; brush several times weekly with slicker brush

Nails: trim once every 6 to 8 weeks or as needed

Exercise: provide plenty of space to run around in a secure environment

Outdoors: be cautious in temperatures over 85°F (29.44°C); provide water and shade

a.) Holding Your Rabbit

When you first bring your rabbit home you should give it a day or two to get used to the new environment before you try to hold it.

When you feel your rabbit is ready, offer it a few treats to encourage the rabbit to approach you on its own. Once your rabbit approaches you, begin petting it gently on the back and ears. If your rabbit responds well to this treatment you can try picking it up. Make sure to support your rabbit's feet and hold the rabbit's body against your chest. As it grows older be sure to keep its feet facing down toward the ground and ensure that its spine is straight.

You will have to judge if your Flemish Giant like to be carried based on his temperament and preferences. Like all rabbits, if handled wrongly or recklessly it can become fearful and sometimes aggressive.

b.) Introducing Your Rabbit to Children

Flemish Giant Rabbits have a wonderful disposition and are great with children, but you need to educate them to be extremely careful and respectful, especially with very young children or it could result in accidental injury.

Before you bring your rabbit home, make sure to talk to your children about the responsibilities of their new pet. Having given your rabbit time to acclimate to its new surroundings, you can try introducing it to your kids. If it is happy for you to do so, hold the rabbit securely in your arms and let your child pet it gently. If your rabbit is calm, you can try setting it down on the ground so your child can pet it.

Do not let very young children handle the rabbit but let them stroke it gently. Teach older children how to properly hold the baby rabbit and how to be careful when putting it back down. Warn them that the rabbit might be frightened by loud noises. As the rabbit grows, they will get very heavy and it is not recommended that children attempt to lift them for if done wrong, the rabbit might use its strong hind legs and claws to protect itself.

c.) Shedding in Rabbits

Some rabbits shed more than others but most breeds shed every three months. Like cats, rabbits are very clean animals and they like to groom themselves. Unlike cats, however, rabbits cannot vomit – thus, if they consume too much hair it could form a ball in the stomach and cause serious health problems. Please see Chapter Six regarding keeping healthy for more information regarding Wool Block.

Due to its size, the Flemish Giant Rabbit Does have more of a challenge in grooming as they can't reach all the parts of their bodies compared to smaller breeds. This is where your assistance is required. In order to help keep their coat smooth and healthy which is a short hair, you should use a slicker brush several times a week to remove loose and dead hair. During shedding seasons in spring and fall, you may need to brush them once a day or even multiple times a day to keep up.

6.) Planning for the Unexpected

If something happens to you, you want to know that your rabbit and any other pets will be properly cared for and loved. Some cell phones allow you to input an ICE (In Case of Emergency) number with notes. If your cell phone has such an option, use it. If it does not, write the following information on a piece of a paper and put it in your wallet with your driver's license:

- The names of each of your pets, including your rabbit.

- The names and phone numbers of family members or friends who have agreed to temporarily care for your pets in an emergency.

- The name and phone number of your veterinarian.

Be sure to also talk with your neighbors, letting them know how many pets you have and the type of pets. That way, if something happens to you, they can alert the authorities, ensuring your pets do not linger for days before they are found.

If you fail to do that and something happens to you, someone will find your rabbit and any other pets and will need to know what to do to ensure that they are cared for. It is a good idea in the case of an emergency, to ask several friends or family members to be responsible for taking care of your pets should something happen to you. Prepare instructions for the intended guardians, providing amended instructions as necessary. Also, if you are happy to do so, be sure to provide each individual with a key to your home (remember to inform your home insurance company so that this does not affect your coverage).

Instructions should include:

- The name and phone numbers of each individual who agreed to take care of your rabbit and other pets.

- Your pet's diet and feeding schedule.

- The name and phone number of your veterinarian.

- Any health problems and medications your rabbit may take on a daily basis, including dosage instructions, instructions on how to give the medicine, and where the medicine is kept.

Put as much information as necessary to ensure the guardians can provide the same level of care to which your rabbit is accustomed.

Chapter Ten: Frequently Asked Questions

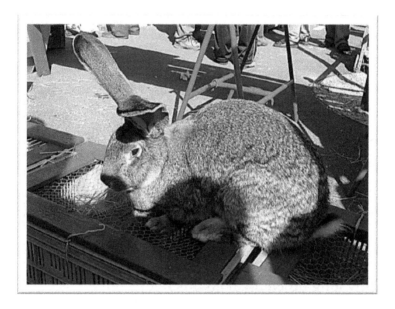

Throughout this book, I've provided information on all aspects of Flemish Giant Rabbit care. You may, however, find yourself with specific questions that need to be answered when you do not feel like skimming through the entire book. If you are in need of a certain tidbit of information, or if you are simply curious about what other rabbit owners want to know, this is the place to look.

In this chapter, I've brought together some of the most frequently asked questions regarding Flemish Giant

Rabbits, along with their answers which I trust will be of assistance to you. If what you need is not there, then please refer to the various websites I've listed in the next chapter.

Q: What are the health benefits of spaying/neutering?

A: Some rabbits exhibit behavioral changes if they are not spayed or neutered -- they may become more aggressive and they may spray urine. For female rabbits, spaying greatly reduces the risk for uterine cancer. Uterine cancer is one of the most common causes of death in un-spayed rabbits and it is often untreatable by the time a diagnosis is made. Neutering male rabbits will help prevent them from fighting with other rabbits which could also serve to extend their lives.

Q: How long do Flemish Giants live?

A: Due to their size, Flemish Giants do not live as long as other domestic rabbit breeds – generally 5 to 7 years, though some have been known to live longer.

Q: What precautions should I take when buying from a breeder?

A: You should take the same precautions in buying from a breeder as you would in a pet store or shelter. You will need to examine the individual rabbits to make sure they are healthy before you even begin to talk about purchasing one. In addition to checking the health of the stock, you should also determine the breeder's experience and credentials. Ask the breeder questions to determine how much they know about the breed, how much experience they have and whether or not they have the required license or registration to breed rabbits legally.

Q: Can I build my own rabbit cage?

A: Yes, you can build your own rabbit cage as long as you use the appropriate materials and make it the right size. The easiest way to make your own rabbit cage is to use stackable wire cubes to create a multi-level cage. However, wire floors can harm the feet of a Flemish Giant more so than smaller house rabbits due to their increased weight so a resting board may be required to prevent him getting sore hocks. Therefore, insert wooden dowels through the gaps in the wire to create supports for a wooden shelf which you can then line with towels and other bedding material to make it more comfortable for your rabbit.

Q: How long does it take Flemish Giant Rabbits to become fully grown?

A: Large breeds of rabbit can take between 8 to 10 months to mature but the Flemish Giant Rabbit may take even longer – A Doe may not become fully mature until 1 year and a Buck make take 1.5 years or older.

Q: What are the benefits of adopting an adult rabbit?

A: Many people prefer to buy baby rabbits because they want to raise the rabbit themselves. While this is a wonderful experience, there are also several unique benefits involved in adopting an adult rabbit. Adult rabbits are more likely to already be litter trained which will save you the hassle of having to do it yourself. It is also more likely that the rabbit will already be spayed or neutered because this is a policy most shelters enforce. Adopting an adult rabbit may also be a little cheaper than buying a baby rabbit from a pet store or breeder.

Q: Can I let my rabbit play outside?

A: Yes, you can let your rabbit play outside as long as you take a few precautions. First, it is important that your rabbit receives all the necessary vaccinations to keep him protected against disease. Second, you should build or buy an outdoor rabbit run that will keep your rabbit safe while he is outside. Even while your rabbit is confined to the run you should keep an eye on him.

You should also be aware that Flemish Giant Rabbits do not handle heat well. Do not take your rabbit outside if it is very hot and, when you do take him out, make sure he has plenty of water and shade to protect him from the sun. Anything over 85°F (29.44°C) can be dangerous.

Q: What kind of special care do Flemish Giants require?

A: In addition to a large cage to accommodate their size, Flemish Giants also need special flooring for their cages. This breed is particularly susceptible to developing sore hocks so they need a solid cage floor with plenty of bedding. Flemish Giants also require a diet slightly higher in protein than other domestic rabbits to support their growth.

Q: How often should I clean my rabbit's cage?

A: The best answer to this question is "as often as necessary". Flemish Giant Rabbits are particularly prone to a disease called Sore Hocks which results, in part, from unclean bedding (in addition to abrasive wire flooring). Generally, you should plan to change your rabbit's bedding once a week but you may need to clean the litter box two or three times within that same period of time.

Q: What vaccinations are required for my rabbit?

A: Vaccinations are not required but certain ones are highly recommended. The two most important vaccines for rabbits are against myxomatosis and viral hemorrhagic disease (VHD) and are recommended in the UK. Both of these diseases are very serious and often fatal. Aside from preventive vaccination, treatments for these diseases are typically ineffective.

Q: Do I need to have my rabbit examined by a vet?

A: Again, it is your choice whether or not you provide your rabbit with routine veterinary care. Some rabbit owners prefer to save themselves the expense of veterinary visits while others see the value in it. The benefit of taking your rabbit in for regular check-ups is that you can catch diseases and conditions in the early stages and provide treatment.

Q: Can I move the babies from the nest box to clean it?

A: No. If you observe the female rabbit you will notice that she never moves the babies from the nest box. When baby rabbits are born they are virtually hairless so they depend on the nest box and their collective body heat to survive. If you move the baby rabbits from the nest box, they could die from exposure. Flemish Giant Rabbits do tend to grow quickly, however, so do not be worried if the babies start to move outside the nest on their own after only a week or so.

Q: Is there a maximum size for Flemish Giants?

A: Though most Flemish Giants top out around 18 lbs. (8.16 kg), it is not unheard-of for them to grow much larger. The maximum size for your Flemish Giant will depend on its genetics – if it comes from larger stock, it may outgrow the "average" maximum size for the breed.

Q: Why can't I give baby rabbits vegetables?

A: While your rabbits are still babies, their bodies are very delicate and sudden changes can cause serious problems. When they are born, baby rabbits do not have the ability to digest solid food – that is why they rely on their mother's milk. As your rabbit grows, however, its stomach will develop. You do not want to feed your baby rabbits vegetables too early, however, or it could give them diarrhea.

Q: How do I keep an outdoor rabbit cool?

A: If you must keep your Flemish Giant outdoors, take some precautions to keep him from overheating. Make sure the hutch is in a location that doesn't receive direct sunlight and keep a portion of the hutch enclosed so it will stay cool. During particularly hot days you can place frozen water bottles inside the hutch for your rabbits to lean against.

Q: How long can I keep breeding my rabbits?

A: Flemish Giants take a little longer to mature than smaller breeds so you may not be able to start breeding them as early. For females, you need to wait until they are 9 months old or 14 lbs. (6.35 kg). You also need to be careful to start breeding before the female is 1 year old because her pelvic bones may fuse after that point, making birthing kits more difficult. Flemish Giant Does shouldn't be bred past the age of 3 because it could increase the chance of dangerous complications during birth.

Q. What about exercise?

A: It is recommended that you give your Flemish Giant some exercise to prevent boredom and from becoming overweight. They can be trained to walk in a harness and due to their size this can be a manageable and realistic option.

Chapter Eleven: Relevant Websites

When you start looking around the internet it can take some time to track down exactly what you are looking for.

Shopping

A one-stop shop for all your rabbit needs is what is required and the sites below offer you the convenience of pulling together many of the best products from around the web. Enjoy Shopping!

United States of America Website
www.rabbitsorbunnies.com

United Kingdom Website
www.rabbitsorbunnies.co.uk

Even after reading this book, you may still have questions or you might be looking for additional information. In this chapter you will find lists of relevant websites in the following topics regarding Flemish Giant Rabbits.

- Feeding Tips
- Care Information
- Health Information
- General Information
- Show Guidelines

1.) Food

These websites will provide you with a wealth of information you need to know about feeding your Flemish Giant Rabbits a healthy diet. You will receive information about your rabbit's nutritional needs, food options and more.

United States Websites:

"Rabbit Diet and Nutrition." Zooh Corner. www.mybunny.org/info/rabbit_nutrition.htm

"Care for and Feeding Your Flemish Giant." GiantGemz Rabbits. http://giantgemzrabbits.webs.com/careandfeeding.htm

"Suggested Vegetables and Fruits for a Rabbit Diet." House Rabbit Society. http://rabbit.org/suggested-vegetables-and-fruits-for-a-rabbit-diet

Krempel, Dana. "What Should I Feed my Bunny?" Miami University. www.bio.miami.edu/hare/diet.html

United Kingdom Websites:

"Feeding and Care." Fieldview Stud, Specialist Breeder.
www.fieldview-rabbits.co.uk/feeding-care.html

"Rabbit – Facts and Care Sheet." Freshfields Animal
Rescue.
www.freshfieldsrescue.org.uk/images/uploads/articles/Rab
bit_care_sheet1.pdf

"Rabbit Feeding and Nutrition." The British Rabbit Council.
www.thebrc.org/feeding.htm

2.) Care

The websites in this section will provide you with all of the
information you need to know about caring for Flemish
Giant Rabbits. You will find information regarding housing
and raising rabbits as well as tips for purchasing a rabbit
from a breeder.

United States Websites:

"Facts and Tips About Raising Flemish Giants." Frank's
Flemish Giants.
http://myplace.frontier.com/~szabof/id7.html

"How Can I Make Sure My Rabbit Wears its Teeth Down?" Pawnation.

http://animals.pawnation.com/can-make-sure-rabbit-wears-its-teeth-down-1575.html

"Rabbit Care." House Rabbit Society.

http://rabbit.org/category/care

"General Rabbit Care." American Society for the Prevention of Cruelty to Animals.

www.aspca.org/pet-care/small-pet-care/general-rabbit-care

United Kingdom Websites:

"Caring For Your Giant Rabbit." Singleton Stud British & Continental Giant Rabbits.

www.british-giantrabbits.co.uk/16_7.html

King, Claire. "Giant Rabbit Care Guidelines."

www.rabbitwelfare.co.uk/pdfs/GiantRabbitCareGuidelines.pdf

"Housing." The British Rabbit Council.

www.thebrc.org/housing.htm

"Caring for Large/Giant Rabbit Breeds." Rabbit Rehome.

www.rabbitrehome.org.uk/care/giantrabbits.asp

3.) Health Information

The websites in this section will provide you with all of the information you need to know about keeping your Flemish Giant Rabbits healthy. You will find information about common health problems, vaccinations and other health-related information.

United States Websites:

"Diseases A-Z: Rabbit." PetMD.
http://www.petmd.com/rabbit/conditions

"Rabbit First Aid Kit." Vortex Hollow Flemish Farm.
https://sites.google.com/site/vortexhollowflemishfarm/home/rabbit-first-aid-kit

"Rabbit Heath." House Rabbit Society.
http://rabbit.org/category/health

"Sore Hocks." OntarioRabbits.org.
http://ontariorabbits.org/health/sore-hocks

"Rabbits Health." Flemish Giants & Co.
http://flemishgiantandcompany.yolasite.com/rabbits-health.php

United Kingdom Websites:

"Health Problems." The British Rabbit Council.
http://www.thebrc.org/health-poblems.htm

"Health." The People's Dispensary for Sick Animals.
www.pdsa.org.uk/pet-health-advice/rabbits/health

 "Rabbits." The Royal Society for the Prevention of Cruelty
to Animals.
www.rspca.org.uk/allaboutanimals/pets/rabbits

4.) General Information

The following websites will provide you with general
information about Flemish Giant Rabbits – here you will
find information regarding the history of the breed, general
facts and owner testimonials.

United States Websites:

"The Flemish Giant Rabbit." RabbitMatters.com.
www.rabbitmatters.com/flemish-giant.html

"Flemish Giant Rabbit." The Maryland Zoo in Baltimore.
www.marylandzoo.org/animals-
conservation/mammals/flemish-giant-rabbit

"Bunny FAQ." LL Rabbit Ranch.

www.llrabbitranch.com/#!faq/cnav

"Varieties." The National Federation of Flemish Giant Rabbit Breeders.

www.nffgrb.net/Varieties.htm

United Kingdom Websites:

"History of the Breed." Fieldview Stud, Specialist Breeder.

www.fieldview-rabbits.co.uk/breed-history.html

"Flemish Giant Breed Profile." PetPlanet.co.uk.

www.petplanet.co.uk/small_breed_profile.asp?sbid=4

"Flemish Giant Rabbit Breed Guide." ClickPets.co.uk.

www.clickpets.co.uk/advice/flemish-giant-rabbit-breed-guide/121

"Flemish Giant Rabbits." The Big Bunny Company.

www.thebigbunnycompany.co.uk/flemish-giant-rabbit

5.) Showing Flemish Giant Rabbits

The following websites will provide you with all of the information you need to know about showing Flemish Rabbits in either the U.S. or the U.K. You will find information regarding the breed standard, how points are awarded and how to prepare for shows.

United States Websites:

Eastern States Flemish Giant Rabbit Breeders Association.
http://esfgrba.webs.com

"ARBA Sanctioned Shows." American Rabbit Breeders
Association, Inc.
www.arba.net/showsSearch.php

"Standards of Perfection for the Flemish Giant Rabbit."
Vortex Hollow Flemish Farm.
https://sites.google.com/site/vortexhollowflemishfarm/hom
e/arba---standards-of-perfection-for-flemish-giant

"Upcoming Shows." The National Federation of Flemish
Giant Rabbit Breeders.
www.nffgrb.net/Shows.htm

United Kingdom Websites:

"Flemish Giant." The British Rabbit Council.
www.thebrc.org/standards/F5-Flemish%20Giant.pdf

"Showing Rabbits." Singleton Stud British & Continental
Giant Rabbits.
www.british-giantrabbits.co.uk/15_29.html

"The BRC Show Diary." The British Rabbit Council.
www.thebrc.org/shows-current-year.htm

"Showing Your Rabbits." Huddersfield & District Fanciers Society.
www.huddersfieldrabbits.org.uk/showingrabbits.htm

Index

D

E

F

G

H

I

K

L

M

N

O

P

W

Photo Credits

By Lucile Petit via Wikimedia Commons,
http://commons.wikimedia.org/wiki/File:Lapin_geant_des_flandres_2.JPG

By Flickr user Romers
www.flickr.com/photos/romers/4618969415

By Richie Graham via Wikimedia Commons,
http://commons.wikimedia.org/wiki/File:Flemish_Giant_2.jpg

By Lucile Petit via Wikimedia Commons,
http://en.wikipedia.org/wiki/File:Lapin_geant_des_flandres
.JPG

By Flickr user The Original Turtle,
www.flickr.com/photos/58638411@N00/4450934757

By Eponimm via Wikimedia Commons,
http://en.wikipedia.org/wiki/File:Geant_des_flandres_101.J
PG

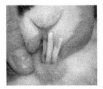

By Uwe Gille via Wikimedia Commons
http://commons.wikimedia.org/wiki/File%3ABradygnathia-
superior-rabbit.jpg

By Ilias 1993 via Wikimedia Commons,
http://en.wikipedia.org/wiki/File:Nest_jonge_Vlaamse_reuz en.jpg

By Gnangarra via Wikimedia Commons,
http://en.wikipedia.org/wiki/File:Rabbit_1hr_old_gnangarr a.jpg

Photo By Lithonius via Wikimedia Commons,
http://en.wikipedia.org/wiki/File:Flemish_giant_fawn_doe.j pg

By Flickr user Mr.TinDC,
www.flickr.com/photos/mr_t_in_dc/2913998754

By Lithonius via Wikimedia Commons,
http://en.wikipedia.org/wiki/File:Sandy_flemish_with_boy.j
pg

By Tangopaso via Wikimedia Commons,
http://en.wikipedia.org/wiki/File:Louhans_G%C3%A9ant-
des-Flandres.jpg

By Stamitisclan via Wikimedia Commons,
http://commons.wikimedia.org/wiki/File:Runt_and_Paxie.j
pg

References

"Bunny FAQ." LL Rabbit Ranch.
www.llrabbitranch.com/#!faq/cnav

"Can I have a pet rabbit?" Department of Agriculture,
Fisheries and Forestry Biosecurity Queensland
http://www.daff.qld.gov.au/__data/assets/pdf_file/0009/577
80/IPA-Keeping-Rabbits-As-Pets-PA15.pdf

"Care and Feeding for Your Giant Flemish Rabbit."
GiantGemz Rabbits.
http://giantgemzrabbits.webs.com/careandfeeding.htm

Coatem, Thomas. "Ancient Origins of the Flemish Giants."
National Federation of Flemish Giant Rabbit Breeders.
www.nffgrb.net/Articles/Ancient%20Origin.htm

"Domestic Baby Bunnies and Their Mom"
www.rabbit.org/care/babies.html

"Facts and Tips About Raising Flemish Giants." Frank's
Flemish Giants.
http://myplace.frontier.com/~szabof/id7.html

"Flemish Giant"
http://en.wikipedia.org/wiki/Flemish_Giant

"Flemish Giant Information." Highland View Rabbitry.
http://highlandviewrabbitry.tripod.com/id26.html

"Frequently Asked Questions." Amanda's Rabbitry.
http://flemishgiantrabbit.webs.com/apps/faq

"Help with Breeding Flemish Giant Rabbits."
Homesteading Today.
www.homesteadingtoday.com/livestock-
forums/rabbits/47952-breeding-flemish-giants.html

"How Can I Make Sure My Rabbit Wears its Teeth Down?"
Pawnation.
http://animals.pawnation.com/can-make-sure-rabbit-wears-
its-teeth-down-1575.html

"Woolblock Prevention"
http://avillionfarm.com/pdflib/RabbitFeedAndWB.pdf

www.threelittleladiesrabbitry.com/woolblock.php

King, Claire. "Giant Rabbit Care Guidelines."
www.rabbitwelfare.co.uk/pdfs/GiantRabbitCareGuidelines.
pdf

"Litterbox Training." BinkyBunny.com.
www.binkybunny.com/BUNNYINFO/tabid/53/CategoryID
/5/PID/940/Default.aspx

"Origins of the Flemish Giants." Thomas Coatoam. The
National Federation of Flemish Giant Rabbit Breeders.
www.nffgrb.net/Articles/Origins.htm

"Rabbit Health." Flemish Giant & Company. http://flemishgiantandcompany.yolasite.com/rabbits-health.php

"The Flemish Giant Rabbit." RabbitMatters.com. www.rabbitmatters.com/flemish-giant.html

"Rabbit Feeding and Nutrition." The British Rabbit Council. www.thebrc.org/feeding.htm

"Rabbit Terms Glossary." Nature Trail. www.thenaturetrail.com/showing-rabbits/terms-glossary

"Veggie List." BinkyBunny.com. www.binkybunny.com/BUNNYINFO/VeggieList/tabid/144/Default.aspx

Notes:

Lightning Source UK Ltd.
Milton Keynes UK
UKHW02f0642181018
330753UK00012B/1137/P